THE HORSEKEEPER'S DAUGHTER

THE HORSEKEEPER'S DAUGHTER

Jane Gulliford Lowes

Matador
9 Priory Business Park,
Wistow Road, Kibworth Beauchamp,
Leicestershire. LE8 0RX
Tel: 0116 279 2299
Email: books@troubador.co.uk
Web: www.troubador.co.uk/matador
Twitter: @matadorbooks

ISBN 978 1788039 741

British Library Cataloguing in Publication Data.
A catalogue record for this book is available from the British Library.

Printed on FSC accredited paper
Printed and bound in Great Britain by 4edge Limited
Typeset in 11pt Minion Pro by Troubador Publishing Ltd, Leicester, UK

Matador is an imprint of Troubador Publishing Ltd

"The Horsekeeper's Daughter" is dedicated to the memory of my
grandfather, Jim Groark.
He made me curious about everything.

Acknowledgements

I always wanted to write a book, so I did; however, I am not a historian, nor am I a writer. This is not an academic work – it's simply a story I wanted to tell, a story that I hope others might enjoy. I have used my best endeavours with my historical research but if any of the facts are inaccurate, I bow to those with greater knowledge.

So many people have helped me tell this story, but in particular I wanted to thank the following:

In Australia, Gary Balkin – if I hadn't spotted his article about the Campbells, there would be no book; Catherine and Rob Marsden for their unending kindness and generosity; Bob Campbell for all the help and information he provided, and for showing copies of the letters and photographs to his dad, Jimmy Campbell; Wendy King, who'd already done so much research into the Campbells, for her superb research skills and for the numerous trips to the Queensland State Archive on my behalf; Muriel Shepherd at the Mount Tamborine Historical Society, and Margaret for showing me around the museum; Iain Hollindale for his wonderful book, *Life and Cricket on the Coomera*, for taking me to the Campbell farm and for showing me around Upper Coomera; Ann Rowley for locating the grave site; Coline Murphy for travelling all the way up to see me in Noosa with very helpful information about the Antrim Campbells; Kate Wall for her fabulous photography which inspired the cover of the book (you can see her work at www.thelightchaser.com.au) and Kayla and Cheryl at the Local Studies Unit, City of Gold Coast Libraries, for helping source images of the Campbells and Bignells.

In England, my family, Marcus, Alan, Moira, Geoff and Robert, for their unending patience and support (moral and financial) for yet another of my mad schemes; Merry the spaniel for his constant companionship, being a general pest and draping his ears all over my keyboard; everyone from Seaton Village who helped with information, in particular Beatrice Lewis, Alyson Slater, Joyce Pescod, Joan Hutchinson (nee Boland) and Stafford Linsley for his very helpful comments and lecture notes on the history of Seaham; Brian Slee for historical photos; my late uncle George Clyde, for information about Edie Threadkell and Caroline Street – sadly he passed away before the completion of this book; Ray Armbrister for information about his ancestors and St Mary the Virgin; all friends (you know who you are) who supported me through this project and put up with my endless ramblings and obsession with the story of Sarah Marshall, especially Alison Fawell, Jackie Stoker, and Jill Rose (for keeping me sane). Also, thanks to everyone who assisted in the production of the book, including my editor, Ben Watson; the staff at Durham Records Office/County Library for permission to use extracts from *Troubled Seams* by John McCutcheon; Jennifer Maine for the beautiful hand-drawn maps; and the staff at Matador Books.

Space in the book is limited but you can see more photographs relevant to the story on my website justcuriousjane.com.

Let's do it all again sometime.

Contents

SUNDERLAND

OLD SEAHAM
SEAHAM
SEATON VILLAGE· HARBOUR
EAST RAINTON SEAHAM COLLIERY
WEST
RAINTON DALTON-LE-DALE

DURHAM

BRANCEPETH
TURSDALE
PAGE
BANK COXHOE

BISHOP SEDGEFIELD
AUCKLAND

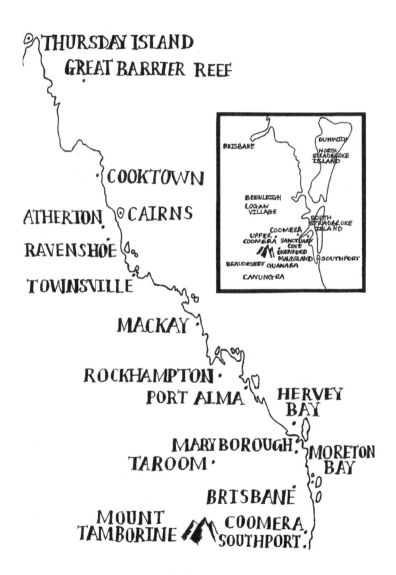

THURSDAY ISLAND
GREAT BARRIER REEF

COOKTOWN

ATHERTON CAIRNS
RAVENSHOE

TOWNSVILLE

MACKAY

ROCKHAMPTON
PORT ALMA   HERVEY
                              BAY

            MARYBOROUGH   MORETON
TAROOM   BAY

            BRISBANE
MOUNT   COOMERA
TAMBORINE   SOUTHPORT

BRISBANE   DUNWICH
                           NORTH
                           STRADBROKE
                           ISLAND

BEENLEIGH
LOGAN
VILLAGE
                    COOMERA   SOUTH
            UPPER   STRADBROKE
            COOMERA SANCTUARY ISLAND
                     COVE
                     OXENFORD
                     MAUDSLAND SOUTHPORT
BEAUDESERT GUANABA

    CANUNGRA

1

Pandora's Box

It's a shabby, tattered old thing, fairly nondescript – the sort of mass-produced, cheap, old attaché case you might find sitting abandoned in the corner of a charity shop or on the bric-a-brac table at the village jumble sale. Designed to look like leather, but in fact made of cardboard, it was stitched around the edges in an attempt to give it an air of quality. The spring had long since sprung from its two catches, which were rusted and stiff. The handle was loose and broken, and the faux leather covering had begun to peel away at the edges several lifetimes ago. Inside, the case was lined with a faded raspberry-pink paper with a geometric design, speckled with brown spots. Both the case and its contents smelled old, musty, the smell of antiquarian bookshops and forgotten memories.

This was Aunt Edie's box. It had always been known as Aunt Edie's box. For at least fifteen years it had lived in the storage compartment under the spare bed, surrounded by old bank statements and revision notes and rolls of wrapping paper. Once every few years, usually while looking for something else, I would stumble across it, and spend half an hour or so looking through its contents – faded old photographs of vanished histories, of people I never knew and whose stories meant nothing to me. Letters, official documents, birth certificates, marriage certificates, death certificates, even wills; all that remained of the entire lives of long-dead strangers.

Aunt Edie wasn't my aunt at all. In fact, she wasn't anybody's aunt. Edie was one of those elderly ladies, known to all and beloved by most, a close friend of the family, who had, it seemed to me, been around forever. She was a friend to my great-grandmother, my grandmother and my mother. And they all called her Aunt Edie. "Aunt" – a term of affection, a badge of honour, a title denoting ties of love and friendship where ties of blood do not exist. Is this a particularly North-Eastern thing, like stotties and plodging and proggy mats and ha'way? Growing up, I had numerous aunties, none of whom were even slightly related, but who were all close friends of my mother and grandmother.

Edie was a tall, stout woman with a kind face, a high-pitched gentle voice and thick ankles. She was one of those sorts of women who had always been old. Dressed in a housecoat and apron and slippers – at least that's how I remember her – she lived in a downstairs flat on a small housing estate in Seaham Harbour, between the railway line, the colliery and the sea, and was very deaf. Her house was full of curious knick-knacks and memories and every time I visited her I would ask to see the box. Off Edie would shuffle to the back room to fetch it. As a child I was fascinated with the "olden days" and would spend hours listening to my grandparents' tales of growing up in Seaham Harbour in the 1920s and 30s. Edie's little attaché case was a treasure trove to me. It was Pandora's box.

Two photographs in particular captured my imagination. The first was of an elderly lady with a gentle smile, dressed in heavy, black Victorian garb, hands placed on a book upon her knees, her white hair tucked up in a pointed bonnet. As a very small girl I always thought she must have been a witch, though perhaps a kindly one. The second, a small sepia photograph with crimped and crumpled edges, of a group of Sunday School children, dressed in their Sunday best with unsmiling faces and frilly bonnets, with the date in the bottom corner – 26th May 1912. I often wondered who these children were and how Edie came to have this photograph. There were vague mentions of "relatives in Australia" but she couldn't really remember.

It was my fascination with this photograph that would ultimately take me on a journey through a hundred and thirty-five years of history, as I uncovered an incredible and unexpected tale of hardship, bravery, love, loss, tragedy and coincidence, of ordinary people enduring extraordinary circumstances.

Some years after Edie passed away, the box came into my possession. Whilst researching my own family tree, I resolved to check the box to see if it contained any photographs of my grandparents, or my mother as a child. It didn't. For the first time, I began to pay proper attention to its contents, and spent an afternoon sorting through the collection of photographs which spanned a hundred years. Gentlemen in uniform with mutton chop whiskers; children in starched pinafores; stony-faced women in Edwardian dress; numerous wedding photos of smiling couples from the 1920s to the 1970s; groups of middle-aged ladies on bus trips to Blackpool, laughing and smiling, all wearing hats and wielding incredibly large handbags. The names of these people had been lost forever. There was not a name, a note or a date, nothing to identify the subjects, nothing which might tell their stories.

There was one small brown envelope containing letters and photographs which differed from all the rest. It was addressed to *"Miss Edith Threadkell, 6 Caroline Street, Seaham Harbour, Co. Durham, UNITED KINGDOM"*. On the back of each of the photographs, faintly written in faded brown ink, were names, dates, places, and detailed descriptions, each one signed either "Bill" or "Topsy".

Whenever I took out Edie's box and began to look through the contents, my fascination and curiosity were always tinged with regret. These letters, these photographs, these reminiscences, they didn't belong to me. I did not recognise in the faces that looked back at me any familiar features; nothing but the smiles of strangers, no recognisable family characteristics, no "you have your great-grandad's eyes". I thought of my own family and my treasured memories of my grandparents, and the photographs and tales of their forbears, all carefully collated and cared for and loved. I felt sad for these long dead souls, ten thousand miles away. And then it became obvious to me. These items had come into my possession not by coincidence but for a clearly defined purpose. There was a story here, a story which was demanding to be unearthed and told. Who were these people and what was their connection to Edie and to Seaham?

In all, there are twenty-five photographs and two letters, written by Bill and Topsy Campbell to Edie in the first six months of 1936. The photographs span the period from 1912 to 1936, and were taken mainly around and upon Tamborine Mountain in South-Eastern Queensland. A man and a woman sitting in a horse-drawn cart, a baby on the young woman's lap; the same couple in their Sunday best, sitting proudly on the veranda of their homestead with their new baby; a man ploughing a field with horses; two small children wandering through the bush; a family group, on the same veranda, years later, the children all grown up; and then the subject and the setting of the photographs seemed to change. No more pastoral scenes, no more smiling family groups. In their place were photographs of the same moustachioed man, plumper, older, careworn, tired, at his work in the far north of Queensland, axe in hand, in the depths of the rainforest.

The photographs and letters stopped abruptly in 1936.

I must have read the letters a dozen times over, scouring the pages for details of names and dates and clues I had missed. Although Bill Campbell's letters listed his children and even their birthdays, my initial enquiries drew a blank. Endless internet searches revealed no information at all. I tried names, birthdates, places, all with the same result. I began to wonder if the details Bill had written were incorrect – was he somehow mistaken (as fathers sometimes are) about his children's dates of birth? Were the names he described actual names or just the children's nicknames? For that matter, I could find no trace of Bill or his unusually-named wife Topsy. My task seemed an impossible one, the obstacles of time and distance too great. Edie's box returned to its place beneath the spare bed, amongst the old photo albums and other possessions I no longer needed but that sentiment would not allow me to part with.

There they remained, for a decade, forgotten.

I have no idea what made me suddenly think of the Campbells again after all those years. In January 2016, on a Tuesday morning, I was sitting at my desk in my large basement office in a stately Victorian terrace in Sunderland, the sort of street which is lined with the once grand houses of doctors, shipping agents, "the middling sort", now populated with solicitors' offices and orthodontists. My view is an uninspiring one, of iron railings and damp mossy brickwork sprouting ferns, litter and the legs of people queuing at the bus stop. On my desk lay sheaves of legal documents, correspondence, medical records, each case an indictment of the industrial heritage that built the city. Shipyard workers slowly dying of mesothelioma, fabricators and welders with hands rendered useless due to years of exposure to vibration from the tools of their trade. I glanced up from my work, distracted by a seagull picking at a discarded fast food wrapper caught in the railings and suddenly thought, "I need to find Bill Campbell."

That evening I retrieved Edie's box and set out the photographs and letters on the floor before me. Bill, with his bushy moustache and a twinkle in his eye, was as charming as I remembered. I took out of the envelope his crumpled old letters, and unfolded his fragile old words. At once familiar and strange, my memories of his stories began to return. With renewed purpose, I resumed the task I had begun ten years before.

My search revealed nothing. Not a hint, not a birth certificate, not an obituary. Not a trace. It appeared there were as many Campbells in Queensland as there were in Glasgow. I decided to take another tack. One of the photographs showed two young girls, maybe twenty years old or so, stood on either side of a handsome young man. On the back of the photograph was written "Jean and Kathleen with Jean's husband, JH Balkin of Gunalda". Balkin. An unusual name. I entered his details online and there it was – the marriage of Jean and Jimmy Balkin, Queensland, 1932.

This was the gateway, the key to the Campbells. I followed the Balkins through trade directories and electoral rolls as they moved around southern Queensland, from the 1930s to the 1960s, and had children of their own, including a son, Gary. After hours of searching, I stumbled upon an article in the *New Farm Village Magazine* (December 2015) by one Gary Balkin.

I opened up the article and couldn't quite believe my eyes. There looking back at me was Bill Campbell – a photograph of Bill winning a logging competition at a country fair in Queensland in 1917 – young, handsome, in his prime, bristling with pride and muscles. The original of that photograph was lying on the floor next to me. I poured over the article, hungry for information, devouring every detail. I contacted the magazine's editor that same evening, asking if he could put me in touch with Gary. I hoped for but didn't expect a response. When I awoke the next day, there was an email from Gary – curious, delighted, fascinated.

I had found the Campbells of Tamborine Mountain and I thought my task was almost at an end. I couldn't have been more wrong. As I delved further into the Campbell family history, I began to unearth a story that weaves back and forth between Seaham and Queensland for decades, a saga of industrial unrest, destitution, adventure, opportunity, love, tragedy, bankruptcy, grief – and one mind-blowing coincidence.

2

Coal Dust

Over the subsequent days and weeks, emails and photographs and information began to flood in from Bill's grandchildren and assorted descendants, and I began to piece together the story of the lives of Bill and Topsy. The answers to some questions still eluded me. What was the link between Bill and Edie? How did a spinster living in a small mining town on the Durham Coast come to have all of these photographs and letters? Why were they so important to her that she had kept them for a lifetime, locked away in a battered old box?

I knew my story would ultimately end in Australia, but for the answers I sought I had to look much closer to home.

Edith Threadkell was born in Seaham Harbour, County Durham on 20th September 1906, the second but only surviving child of Robert Threadkell, a mariner, and his wife, Fanny Hood Threadkell (nee Marshall). Edie was a plain-looking child, devoted to her mother – Robert was absent from the family home for months, sometimes years at a time, away at sea serving with the Merchant Navy. Edie saw little of him as she grew up, at least until his retirement from the seafaring life at the end of the First World War.

The relationship between Robert and Fanny was perhaps an unusual one. Robert, who was born into a seafaring family in Woodbridge, Suffolk on 10th January 1853, had married Fanny in the County Durham port of South Shields in April 1904. She was twenty-two and worked as a housekeeper at the lodging house in Oyston Street, South Shields, where Robert stayed when his ship docked in the Tyne ports. Robert was twenty-nine years older than Fanny. Both their ages are incorrectly recorded on their marriage certificate. Robert was fifty-one, not fifty; Fanny was twenty-two, not twenty-three. What brought them together? Perhaps financial necessity – a girl in domestic service and from a poor family was unwise to turn down a proposal from a gentleman with a secure income in those days; perhaps a genuine affection for one another. In reality, it was most likely a combination of the two. Certainly, this was no marriage of convenience and produced two children, one of whom died in infancy, the other, Edie.

When I visited Edie as a child with my mother and younger brother, Edie would bring out of the china cabinet a heavy trinket box, made simply out of rough wood, varnished and painted with an image of a ship in full sail on the lid. As children, we had always referred to it as the "Sea Captain's Box" because it had been made by Robert Threadkell on one of his voyages. Whether Robert ever actually captained a ship is unknown but it seems unlikely – there is no record of him ever having done so. The box was full of brass buttons and old coins – copper pennies and thre'penny bits – the sort of things small children enjoy sorting and playing with – but it also contained Robert's service medals from the war and various other tokens. When Edie died, the box passed into the possession of my younger brother, another Robert, and he has it still.

Robert Threadkell's marriage to Fanny Marshall was not his first. As a young man, he'd married Ellen Kinross, from Seaham Harbour and they'd had three children, Isabella, Maria and Elizabeth. Their descendants, Currys and Hudsons, still live in the town. Ellen died in October 1893 aged forty two. Elizabeth, their youngest daughter, was only three years old at the time. How Robert had met Ellen and why he had chosen to settle in Seaham Harbour is unclear. Perhaps his ship was a regular visitor at the small but busy harbour here.

Seaham. Where to begin? How is it possible to describe with objectivity the town where I grew up and have lived almost my entire life? I have loved and hated this place, in equal measure. A small former mining town of some twenty-two thousand souls, it clings to the Durham coastline, battered by the North Sea, surrounded by farm land and bordered by the two ancient villages of Seaton (known locally as, simply, "the Village") to the north-west and Dalton-le-Dale to the south-east.

I have longed to escape this town. I have yearned to return. Wherever I travel in the world, it calls me back like a fretful lover. In my younger days, I was desperate to get away. As a child and then a teenager, I despised its shabby, run-down main street, the endless brick-built terraces and sprawling council estates, the town's three collieries, which were its lifeblood, the coal-stained beaches, the small-town mentality and its narrow-minded people.

As an adult, my perceptions have changed. And so has my town. Today, Seaham is a busy, thriving, pleasant place, which its people are proud to call home, a location outsiders want to visit. Visitors flock here, perhaps whiling away a few hours on the sandy beach, investigating the rock pools, hunting for sea glass, or people-watching sitting at one of the seafront cafes, maybe visiting the lifeboat museum and the attractive little marina.

There is now no sign of the coal industry which created the town and provided employment for thousands of its sons for one hundred and fifty years, no clue left behind of Seaham's industrial heritage, save for the occasional smudge of coal dust in the sand and in the lungs of those who remember some other life. Where there were once pit shafts and spoil heaps and railway tracks, there are now executive houses, nature reserves, cliff-top walks, rare orchids and picnic spots. The town even boasts a five-star hotel with a luxury spa, beloved of footballers and visiting pop stars. This miraculous transformation has occurred in a single generation.

I have fallen in love with the very place I detested and

9

with its warm-hearted and generous people. Shame has been usurped by pride. It's not just the town that has changed. I have too.

For two decades, I have lived in a house overlooking the pretty village green and the manor house in Seaton. The Village predates the main town of Seaham by centuries. There has been a settlement here probably since Roman times – a hoard of Roman coins was unearthed in the village stream a century or more ago – but the village itself has existed for perhaps a thousand years.

In many ways Seaton is the archetypal English north-country village, with its white-washed houses and farmsteads clustered around the small green, and overlooking it all, the village pub, the Dun Cow. For over one hundred and sixty years, the Dun Cow has been the centre of village life. Officially voted the best country pub in County Durham by CAMRA in 2016, unofficially it's the best pub in the world. Log fires, real ales, live music, no food, no jukebox. It's the kind of pub where you have to step over several dogs to get to the bar, where every patron will announce his arrival to those already present with the standard greeting in these parts – "Alreet?" Strangers don't remain strangers for long – within ten minutes of crossing the threshold and ordering a pint of Northumbrian Blonde, you can expect to be interrogated by locals who will extract your entire life story and declare that you must in some way be related.

Although the village has changed significantly in the last thirty to forty years, with new houses on the periphery where farmyards and barns once stood, it has never lost its character. Or its characters. And there are plenty of those. There are still farmers in the village, but it's now largely populated by teachers, solicitors, doctors, police officers, businessmen and the occasional Premier League footballer. My house stands on the site of the barns which formed part of Village Farm; the close of houses of which it is a part, follows the layout of the old farmyard. The Village Farmhouse is still there, yards from the pub, a six-bar-gate's width from my home, and still occupied after two hundred and fifty years or so.

Despite the metamorphosis of Seaham in my lifetime, there remains much that Robert Threadkell and his daughter Edie would have recognised.

The modern town is in fact made up of a number of older villages – Old Seaham, the original ancient hamlet, of which nothing remains but the beautiful Saxon church of St Mary the Virgin, its vicarage and Seaham Hall, now a luxurious hotel; half a mile to the south, Seaham Harbour, constructed to export coal from the Marquis of Londonderry's County Durham coal mines at Rainton; New Seaham, a mile or so inland, the mining village which sprung up around Seaton (later Seaham) Colliery, and the two agricultural villages of Seaton and Dalton-le-Dale which, due to their respective locations (on top of a hill and in a small valley), have retained their separate identities.

Old Seaham had existed for at least a thousand years when Sir Ralph Milbanke constructed Seaham Hall on the site of Seaham Cottage in 1792. The tiny Saxon church, with its flag of St George permanently aflutter in the stiff sea breeze, is overlooked by so many passers-by. It is well worth a visit. The churchyard is filled with the bones and the names of parishioners from Seaton Village, for which it served as parish church long after Old Seaham disappeared – Thompsons, Hodgsons, Bolands.

When I was a child I visited the graveyard around the church, searching for the pirate's grave, so-called because it was carved with a skull and crossbones. Whether it ever actually belonged to a pirate is highly unlikely, but it certainly captured my imagination. The village is described in detail by Elizabeth Grant, the daughter of the Scottish Laird of Rothiemurchus, born in 1797, in her *Memoirs of a Highland Lady*. The book, published in 1898, three years after her death, includes recollections of childhood visits to Seaham, playing on the beach and making necklaces of seaweed, rose-covered cottages, the surrounding farms, and paints an idyllic scene.

11

Seaham Hall itself is an imposing white Georgian pile, perched on the cliff tops overlooking the North Sea, surrounded by lawns where the old village once stood, with terraced gardens sloping down to the wooded dene on its southern aspect. It is perhaps most famous for being the location of the wedding of the famous poet and infamous society dandy George Gordon, Lord Byron to Anne Isabella (known as Annabella) Milbanke, Sir Ralph's daughter, in 1815, and the couple lived there for a short time after their wedding. I've always been quite entertained by the fact that the civic authorities in Seaham have done so much to try to preserve the memory of its most illustrious resident. Over the years we've been blessed with a Lord Byron's Walk, a Byron Terrace, a Byron Terrace School, a Byron Lodge Estate, and most latterly, Byron Place, a small, ugly, soulless shopping centre constructed of steel and glass, overlooking the busy docks and the grey North Sea beyond.

Byron lived here less than a year and is rumoured to have detested the place. It could not have been further from his debauched, high-society celebrity lifestyle, his numerous lovers and his fancy London literary friends, and he couldn't escape from the place fast enough.

It appears that Byron quickly grew to detest Annabella, having married more for money than love, and their marriage lasted barely a year, although it did produce a daughter. Ada, Countess of Lovelace (known today simply as Ada Lovelace), was something of a prodigy and became a famous mathematician, working with Charles Babbage on one of the world's first computers, the mechanical Analytical Engine. In January 1816, Byron turfed Annabella and their child out of their Piccadilly home, making some excuse about having to sell the house because of financial difficulties. Annabella and Ada travelled to Leicestershire to stay with her parents; Annabella never saw him again. Eventually Byron famously fled to Europe and his beloved Greece, where he joined the War of Independence. He died aged thirty four of fever at Missolonghi in 1824, a national hero to the Greek people.

I imagine he's spinning in his grave at the thought of the local populace celebrating his memory by popping into Greggs in Byron Place for a steak bake and a cheese pasty. Byron, a man who devoted his entire life to the pursuit of pleasure, would have, however, been more impressed by the fact that his former home is now a luxury five-star hotel, complete with oriental spa and outdoor hot tubs. There's a delicious irony in the fact that guests at the hotel can trample at will over Byron's most famous works. Quotes from his poems are woven into the very fabric of the carpet which sweeps along the upper corridors and down the grand staircase...

"She walks in beauty like the night... Upstairs, to the right, and into the ladies' powder room."

Or something along those lines.

The rural idyll described by Elizabeth Grant and experienced by Byron did not persist for long after the poet's departure. After his new son-in-law had worked his way through a fair proportion of the family money, and in dire financial straits as a result of funding his own political campaigns, Sir Ralph was forced to sell his estates. In 1821, Seaham Hall and the surrounding land was sold off to Lord Charles William Vane, Baron Stewart at that time and British Ambassador to Vienna, who would shortly become the Third Marquis of Londonderry, mine-owner and industrialist, after his elder brother and heir to the title slit his own throat.

The fate of the hamlet was sealed, the industrial revolution finally arrived and Old Seaham was changed forever. Coal was now king. In the words of a local historian

> *"The Black Death of the pit... was spreading eastwards like the plague."* [1]

---

1   *Troubled Seams, a County Durham Mining Narrative in the 19th Century*, John McCutcheon, Seaham, 1955 p.29. Durham County Record Office DC/ALM 4/10. Reproduced by permission of Durham County Record Office.

The town's street names and public buildings still bear testimony to the Marquis and his family – Londonderry Street, Castlereagh Road, The Londonderry Institute, Viceroy Street, Tempest Road, and the Londonderry Offices which for many years served as the town's police station and which are now luxury flats overlooking the harbour; the Vane Tempest Colliery was named in memory of his second wife Frances-Anne Vane Tempest, a teenage heiress and society belle who owned land and collieries throughout the county. However, the Third Marquis was a tyrant and ruled his estates and his business interests with a rod of iron, seeking assistance from the Home Secretary to suppress the fledgling "Union of Pitmen" in 1826. In 1844, during the four-month-long strike by the Northumberland and Durham miners, the Marquis wrote the famous "Seaham Letter", forbidding local tradesmen and shopkeepers to extend credit or any other form of assistance to the impoverished strikers. The Third Marquis died in 1854, and the formidable Frances Anne took control of his land, estates and industrial concerns, choosing to live at Seaham Hall rather than her country estates or London mansion.

Coal mining created the town of Seaham, and as I delved deeper into Edie's past searching for a connection to the Campbells of Tamborine Mountain, I began to discover that her story and that of Bill and Topsy Campbell had their beginnings in the Londonderry-owned collieries and villages of County Durham.

It was then that I stumbled upon an incredible coincidence for which I was totally unprepared.

3

The Girl Next Door

Amongst the photographs in Edie's box, there was one to which I had not paid much attention. It isn't a portrait, a family group or even an attractive landscape, and so I had merely glanced at it and cast it aside on the pile of anonymous faces. One cold winter evening, sitting on the floor in front of my wood stove, I took out the box and began to re-read Bill's correspondence for what seemed the hundredth time. Bill's words were now so familiar to me I could recite parts of his letters in my head. Frustrated, I felt no nearer to finding the connection between Edie and Bill than when I'd started. I folded up the letters and placed them back in their old brown paper envelope. As I did so, on the top of the pile of pictures and Robert Threadkell's will, my attention was drawn to the photograph I had discarded.

It's a very boring photograph, in black and white, of a single plain white gravestone. Nothing fancy, arched at the top and surrounded by low rectangular wrought iron railings. There are no flowers or shrubs, and the unkempt patch of ground within the railings is covered with rocky soil. The cemetery in the middle of the Queensland Bush in which the grave lies looks overgrown, neglected, perhaps even abandoned. The simple inscription on the gravestone reads:

"In Loving Memory Of
Sarah Campbell
Gone but not forgotten"

No "loving mother of", no "beloved wife of" – there was nothing to link this poor soul to any other person, living or dead.

I turned over the photograph and there in the faded familiar longhand I now recognised as Topsy's were the matter-of-fact words, *"This is Willie's mother's grave. This photo isn't a very good one, the sun was too hot for the camera."* Then, intriguingly, *"For Grannie and you xxx."*

Willie? Who was Willie Campbell? Why was Topsy sending a photograph of this woman's grave to Edie and her grandmother? What a bizarre thing to send to someone ten thousand miles away.

Then of course it dawned on me – Willie Campbell and Bill Campbell were one and the same person. But what of his mother Sarah Campbell? Where did she fit into the story? Why would Edie and her grandmother Margaret (the old lady in the witch photograph) be interested in seeing a photograph of her grave?

For days, I pondered this conundrum, but the more I thought about it the more I tied myself up in knots.

A few days later I received an email from a lady by the name of Wendy King, from Brisbane. It transpired that a copy of my original email to Gary Balkin had been forwarded to Wendy. Wendy's son Jason was married to one of Bill and Topsy's great-grandchildren, Rebeca Campbell, and Wendy had already spent some time researching the Campbell family tree. Wendy was a godsend and a mine of information; it was she who provided the crucial piece of information that changed everything. Bill's mother, the woman who lay buried in forgotten cemetery, was Sarah Marshall.

Sarah Marshall. Edie's mother Fanny had been a Marshall before her marriage; her grandmother was Margaret Marshall. Sarah was the link between Edie Threadkell and Bill Campbell, the golden thread that connected Seaham and Tamborine Mountain.

Now that I had a name my research began in earnest. My search for information about Sarah Marshall became an obsession. I would spend hours every day pouring over birth, death and marriage certificates, census records and family trees. How was Sarah Marshall connected to Fanny, Margaret and Edie?

In a sudden moment of clarity, I realised that Sarah was Fanny's much older sister. Edie was her niece, and Margaret Marshall her mother. Topsy had sent the photograph to show Margaret her daughter's final resting place, perhaps at Margaret's request, perhaps simply as a kindly gesture. What possible chain of events could have resulted in Sarah Marshall being laid to rest in a seemingly remote country cemetery, thousands of miles away from home?

Sarah Marshall was born on 29th July 1863 in the County Durham mining village of West Rainton, within sight, across the meadows, of the mighty Norman cathedral that towers above the beautiful and ancient university city of Durham. The parish church of St Mary the Virgin, in which Sarah was baptised on 29th November 1863, still stands, its lofty spire visible from miles around. Sarah's parents, Thomas and Margaret Marshall, were itinerant mining folk who had come to Rainton from elsewhere in the county to work in Lord Londonderry's Rainton pits. Thomas, a Yorkshireman, had married Margaret in 1861.

Throughout the nineteenth and early twentieth century, until the nationalisation of the coal industry in 1947, it was not uncommon for miners and their families to move around from mine to mine; the sinking of a new pit would create a demand for workers, and they would bundle up their families and their few possessions and move on to the next colliery, perhaps in the next village or in the next county, on a promise of better wages. Those involved in the new trade union movement were frequently labelled as troublemakers and blacklisted by colliery owners, sacked and evicted from their mine-owned cottages and forced to move on, sometimes changing surnames as they went, as a man with a "bad name" was likely to find that his reputation preceded him.

My four times great-grandfather, Tom Bamborough, had come from Rainton with his brothers to work on the expansion of the harbour at Seaham for Lord Londonderry in the early 1840s. He and two of his brothers each had a son called Tom, and the three Bamborough cousins were known as Fair Tom, Red Tom and Darkie Tom, distinguished by their hair colour to avoid confusion. Fair Tom, born in 1852, went to work in the Seaham pit, the first of five generations of my forebears to do so. Whether we like it or not, coal is in our blood.

Sarah Marshall was the eldest of seven daughters born to Thomas and Margaret Marshall; there were some twenty years between Sarah and Fanny, Edie's mother, the youngest of the Marshall girls. Little written evidence remains of Sarah's childhood, and certainly no hint of the adventures and trials that lay ahead of her. I decided to search the census records to see what, if anything, I could glean about her there.

In the 1871 census, I found Sarah aged nine, living in Cassop, another mining village a few miles outside of Durham, with her parents Margaret and Thomas Marshall, Margaret's widowed father, other assorted relatives, and two younger sisters Ann and Elizabeth, then aged five and two. Another four sisters would follow in the next eleven years. Thomas' occupation is given as "horsekeeper" – in colliery parlance this meant he looked after the pit ponies.

Pit ponies (usually mules or small horses as opposed to actual ponies) were the living and breathing engines of every coal mine, pulling the laden coal wagons from the coal face to the base of the shaft, which could sometimes be a distance of several miles. These unfortunate animals would often spend their entire working lifetimes underground, permanently blinkered, never seeing daylight, stabled in the bowels of the mine. Theirs was a desperately hard life of burden and toil but in general they were very well looked after and well-fed, as without them a coal mine simply couldn't function. Quite often they worked until they dropped; occasionally, if they were lucky, they might be put out to grass once they were too old to work.

A poorly-paid horsekeeper like Thomas Marshall could expect to be in charge of the welfare of a team of eight to fifteen ponies, and he would be responsible for grooming, washing down and feeding his animals, and would know each one by name. He would also be responsible for a team of drivers, usually teenage boys who led the ponies back and forth from the coal face. The horsekeeper also mucked out the stables and cleaned and dressed the frequent grazes and cuts suffered by his team in the course of their work; many horsekeepers developed a great fondness for their animals, and would bring them apples and carrots or maybe a cube of sugar as a rare treat.

Pit ponies were still used in the mines of County Durham in living memory, though their use was gradually phased out after the coal industry was nationalised and with increased mechanisation. In later years, during the statutory summer holiday "pit fortnight" every July, the ponies would be brought up and put out to grass in nearby fields. My mother remembers watching them galloping and prancing around in the fresh air, temporarily released from their underground prison. "Darkie", the last pit pony at nearby Murton Colliery, was brought to the surface in 1972.

In 1953 there were still over three hundred pit ponies working in the Seaham collieries. My father recalls clearly the overwhelming stench that came from the underground stables at Seaham Colliery where he started work as an apprentice electrician in 1958. At Ryhope, a little way up the coast from Seaham, there is a bronze statue of a pit pony marking the entrance to the village, a memorial to the countless ponies who lived and died for the getting of coal.

In later records, Thomas Marshall is described as a "colliery cartman" and "banksman". The banksman's job was to empty the coal tubs as they arrived on the surface, having been drawn up the shaft from the depths of the mine. He would then weigh the coal and stone and send the empty tubs back down. It was unrelenting, back-breaking, dirty work but at least he was spared the horrors and dangers endured by those who toiled at the coal face.

Each of the Marshall girls had been born in a different village, another indication of the family's itinerant lifestyle, until they appear to have settled in Tursdale near Spennymoor in 1872, a few miles from where Margaret Marshall had been born and raised in Coxhoe.

I could find no further trace of Sarah until the 1881 census.

The census of 1881 was carried out on the night of 11th April. I looked for Sarah in Tursdale where her parents and younger sisters still lived. I looked for her in the surrounding mining villages, of Spennymoor, Coxhoe, Thornley, Page Bank, Brancepeth. And then all of a sudden, there she was, in the place I had least expected. I couldn't quite believe what I was seeing. I read and re-read the manuscript record before me, my heart pounding and my mind racing, convinced that my eyes were deceiving me, that I had made some sort of mistake. I hadn't.

"Sarah Marshall. 19. Place of birth – West Rainton. Domestic Servant in the household of Thomas Boland, Farmer. Village Farmhouse, Seaton Village."[2]

Sarah was the girl next door.

2   England and Wales Census 1881, Seaton with Slingley.

4

Troubled Seams

Occasionally something happens which completely changes our perspective of that which we know and love. It can be something as simple as discovering a new footpath across familiar fields which affords us a fresh view of our homes in the distance. Sometimes it is the discovery of a secret about a dear friend or relative which can deepen or extinguish the bonds between us. Perhaps it is an event or circumstance or coincidence that casts the familiar in an unfamiliar light, the places we have known and loved for a lifetime seen through a different lens.

I was completely stunned by the discovery of the connection between Sarah Marshall's life and my own. She began to occupy my thoughts day and night. In the mornings, I pulled open my grey silk curtains and looked out onto the village green, the manor house with its tree-lined gardens, bordered by ancient brick walls, at the edge. I glanced along the street to the pub, its whitewashed walls, brass lamps, and the words "DUN COW" picked out in gold upon the smart green paintwork, dazzling in the early morning sunshine. I saw with fresh eyes the scene that had greeted me for twenty years – the same scene that would have greeted Sarah one hundred and thirty-five years before as she went about her duties, perhaps feeding the animals in the barn where my house now stands, perhaps hanging out the washing in the same spot as I did, at the top of the farmyard which is now my back garden. At night, I would lie awake for hours, constantly turning over in my mind the information I had stumbled upon. I even began to dream about her.

Sarah Marshall was taking me over, body and soul. She became my obsession. Always, though, I came back to the same question. Why did she go to Australia? What life experiences had she encountered, what things had she witnessed, what hopes and ambitions did she harbour – what factors had combined to cause Sarah to leave her life as a domestic servant in a quiet County Durham village and travel thousands of miles to start a new life on the far side of the world?

I could find no record of Sarah's departure from England to Australia; I didn't even have an approximate date. I knew Bill Campbell had been born in 1892 in Queensland, but that was my only point of reference. There was no clue in Edie's box of treasures, no mention of her in any of the letters or photographs other than the faded photograph of Sarah's final resting place. I was no closer to discovering Sarah's story than when I had first learned of her existence.

I was searching for Sarah in the wrong place. I began to look for her at the end of her journey rather than the beginning. There, recorded amongst the thousands of names of those who had sought out new lives in the colonies in the nineteenth century, in the immigration records and ships' passenger lists in the Queensland State Archive, I found her.[3]

Sarah Marshall had sailed on the SS Duke of Sutherland from London, bound for Brisbane, in the late Autumn of 1886, aged twenty-three. I wondered if perhaps she was newly married, setting out with her husband to seek a new life in a far-off land. However, the records are quite clear. Perhaps unusually for a young woman in those days, Sarah was travelling alone.

Gradually I began to piece together the story of Sarah's life, both in England and in Queensland. As I delved deeper into the history of Seaham and Seaton Village in the 1880s, a surprising

---

3 Queensland State Archive, Immigration Records, *SS Duke of Sutherland* 1886.

picture began to emerge. Far from being a quiet little backwater on the North-East coast, in the 1870s and 1880s the burgeoning town of Seaham was a hotbed of politics and industrial unrest. The Seaton and Seaham of the early 1880s, in particular, was not a happy place to be, scarred forever by the events of 8th September, 1880.

After purchasing Old Seaham and the surrounding land from the Milbankes in 1821, Lord Londonderry had set about creating the harbour at Seaham for the purpose of transporting coal from his pits at Rainton and Pittington; however, he also knew that the surrounding land was rich in coal deposits. The building of the town around the harbour began in 1828, and eventually the town would support three collieries – Seaton (later known as Seaham) sunk in 1845, a mile or so across the fields from the village after which it was named, Dawdon, a half mile or so south of the harbour along the coast (1907), and Vane Tempest (1928) on the cliff tops a half a mile north of the harbour.

Londonderry built the Rainton–Seaham railway line in 1831, linking his collieries with his newly-built port. Nothing of the railway remains – it was dismantled in the 1890s – however, you can still trace part of its path, from Seaton Bank Top, skirting the edge of Scout's Wood and "Darkie's Plantation", crossing the fields just south of Seaton Village over to where Melrose Crescent stands now, and on into the old pit yard. Every day Sarah Marshall would have heard the endless clanking and rattling of the coal wagons back and forth along the railway line as she went about her duties on the farm.

When John McCutcheon wrote his famous book *Troubled Seams – The Story of a Pit and Its People* in 1955, which details the events in this and subsequent chapters, the town's three mines were producing some 1,800,000 tons of coal each year. At that time, it was estimated that some six thousand men were employed in the coal industry, and that some eighty per cent of men in the town were connected directly or indirectly with the coal industry.

Seaham Colliery, known locally as the Nicky Nack and in later years as simply the Nack, was an amalgamation of two collieries, Seaton Colliery, the "High Pit" and Seaham Colliery, sunk in 1849, the "Low Pit". The two collieries were linked together underground in November 1864, as it was considered safer to have two separate shafts in case an accident or explosion blocked one. Among the older generation of Seaham residents, parts of the town are still known by their old names; the Westlea and Eastlea areas are referred to as the High Colliery (there is still a High Colliery Post office); the Low Colliery describes the brick built terraces of colliery houses that run at a ninety-degree angle from Station Road to Christchurch, where I was brought up. Eventually the new village of New Seaham which sprung up around the colliery and the older village of Seaham Harbour, around the port, would merge and become simply, Seaham. The old names still live on – even today, if you happen to be heading to the town's shopping area or seafront, you're going "down the Harbour".

Accidents and explosions, injuries and fatalities were a regular occurrence in 19th century coal mining. For those whose forefathers have not laboured at the coal face and who have no knowledge or understanding of the heavy price that the coal industry took upon the lives of those who toiled, it is difficult to put into words the desperately hard lives of the miners and their families and the conditions in which they worked and lived. Labour was cheap and so were lives. Some five hundred and twenty-seven men and boys perished in a little under a century and half of coal mining in this small town, with fatalities occurring as recently as the late 1980s.[4]

From almost the very beginning, Seaham Colliery had a dangerous reputation, and it soon became known throughout the county as the "Hell Pit". This nickname was well deserved – in 1852 alone there were three separate explosions, with six lives lost in the last. An inquest revealed that naked lights were still

4   Statistics from dmm.org.uk

being used, despite the widespread availability of miner's lamps. One of those killed was a ten-year-old boy, Charles Halliday. His brother escaped.[5] Child labour was of course commonplace, and continued into the early twentieth century. A government enquiry in 1842 had established that children as young as five years old worked underground as trappers, opening and closing the doors situated at intervals from the shafts to the coal face to allow fresh air to flow, for up to sixteen hours a day. My own great-grandfather, John Clyde, first went to work down the mine at Seaham when he was twelve years of age, and worked there all his life, apart from a few years during the First World War when he exchanged the horrors of the coal face for the horrors of the trenches.

A further explosion claimed two lives in 1864, and some twenty-six souls were lost in the horrific events of the explosion on 25th October 1871.[6] Only four bodies were brought out initially – the remaining twenty-two were not recovered for another two months, as the part of the mine where these poor souls lay was sealed off to prevent the risk of further explosions and so that coal production could continue. As far as the colliery owners were concerned, mining had to continue, at any cost.

As a result of these events and others like them in coal mines across the country, not least at Hartley in Northumberland in January 1862 when two hundred and four miners perished, and in response to increasing industrial discontent about safety, pay and conditions, the Durham Miners Association formed in 1869. The North of England Institute of Mining and Mechanical Engineers was created as a direct result of the 1852 explosion, and met for the first time in the Mill Inn, Seaham. The First Miners' Gala took place in Durham City in 1871, creating a tradition that continues today, decades after the last Durham coal mine disappeared.

---

5   *Troubled Seams*, John McCutcheon 1955 DRO DC/ALM 4/10 p. 41.
6   Ibid pp. 66–72.

The infamous Mill Inn holds a special place in the history of the town. It's still there, in a dip at the bottom of three small hills, just below the modern Catholic church of St Cuthbert on the main road to Sunderland. It has passed through a succession of owners in recent years and its whitewashed walls have perhaps seen better days, but it's still going and still serving pints to the locals. The windmill, which gave the inn its name, is long gone, though my mother can still recall it. Mill Road and Mill Cottage, built where the mill once stood, are the only evidence of its existence. The original Mill Inn was probably a coaching inn; the current building was constructed around 1892 and now lends its name to that particular area of the town.

In February 1874, the Mill Inn was the scene of one of the most notorious incidents in the town's history.[7] Growing resentment at the appalling working conditions and the mistreatment of the miners and their families at the hands of the colliery owners, coupled with frustration at a lack of redress, as these poor workers did not even have the right to vote, combined to create a powder-keg atmosphere. At that time, Britain was a two-party state, governed alternately by the Conservatives and Liberals. The Liberal government of William Ewart Gladstone had been in power for a little over five years, and the Conservatives under Benjamin Disraeli won a landslide victory in the 1874 parliamentary elections. However, Durham was a Liberal stronghold and its thirteen parliamentary seats all returned Liberal members. The first election in February 1874 had been extremely tight, with the Liberal, Bell, a Middlesbrough iron manufacturer, being declared the victor with 4364 votes, his fellow Liberal, Palmer, attracting 4327 votes, and the two Conservative candidates Elliot and Pemberton polling 4011 and 3501 votes respectively.

The Conservatives were livid and challenged the election results in the courts on the basis of the events in Seaham on election day. Rioting had occurred on Church Street, near the

---

7   Ibid pp. 73–78.

Harbour, at that time the main shopping thoroughfare of the town, with shop premises being attacked at random and carts overturned. Tar barrels had been set on fire to form a barricade, and extra police were brought in from Castle Eden around seven miles to the south, and a detachment of soldiers from Sunderland were hastily summoned to try to disperse the crowds.

A local magistrate read the Riot Act, but late that evening a group of rioters headed to the far end of the town, past the colliery and attacked the Mill Inn. No one seems to know why the Inn was selected as a target, but the innkeeper, John Barrett Wells, appears to have heard about the rioting elsewhere in town earlier in the day and had locked up and barricaded his premises as a precaution. A group of around forty men laid siege to the inn, throwing rocks through the windows and attempting to use a battering ram on the front door. What followed has been described as like a scene from the American Wild West,[8] with glasses and bottles smashing everywhere and the besieged landlord, Mr Wells, firing on the mob from an upstairs window while his terrified barmaid Ellen Cook escaped by climbing through a skylight and clambering along the roof. The rioters finally began to disperse around midnight as a large group of policemen and special constables approached. Miraculously, no one was killed.

As a result of these events, the Conservatives successfully petitioned the High Court for a fresh election on the basis of intimidation and the election was declared "null and void on account of the general intimidation resorted to". A second election was held on 8th June 1874, and this time Sir George Eliot, a colliery owner and Conservative who had come third in the February election, was victorious. The Siege of the Mill Inn would go down in history, and the Inn bears a blue plaque near the front door in commemoration. Unrest and discontent at pay and conditions continued, but all was overshadowed by what was to come.

Seaton Village stands atop a small hill. To the rear of the

8   Ibid p. 76.

Dun Cow and the farmhouse, the town of Seaham is clearly visible a mile or so away across the fields. Sarah Marshall would have looked out every morning at the colliery in the distance, perhaps greeting those of her neighbours who worked there on their way to start their shift, including the two young Knox boys, John and David, who lived in a small cottage with their parents Eliza Jane and John, in the small square of houses where Redroofs bungalow now stands.

The colliery never slept and production continued twenty-four hours a day. At around half past nine on the night of 7th September 1880, the Knox boys said goodbye to their mother, making their way past the Dun Cow and through the darkness down the familiar coach road, which wound its way towards Seaham, on their way to start their shift at the colliery at ten o'clock.

Neither Sarah nor their mother would ever see them again.

5

Heaven and Hell

On a May Saturday morning, I picked my way through Seaham Hall Dene, towards the ancient church of St Mary the Virgin, with a single purpose in mind. "Dene" seems to be almost exclusively a north-eastern word for a small wooded valley leading down to the sea. It was the sort of sunny-but-nowhere-near-as-warm-as-it-looks day that Mother Nature specialises in around this part of the Durham coast, the sort of morning that deceives you into wearing short sleeves but leaves you yearning for a winter coat as soon as you enter the shade. Knee deep in bluebells and wild garlic, I stumbled off the main footpath and through beds of nettles, descending deeper into the dene, accompanied only by birdsong and the distant crashing of waves on the beach below.

Decades had passed since I was last here and I had forgotten just how beautiful it is. You can follow the dene, a short distance from where Edie Threadkell lived, as it cuts first through fields and then woods, carving its way through the limestone, from the railway line to the sea, snaking past the bottom of the terraced gardens of Seaham Hall, overlooked by the little church high to the left. A green chain-link fence, recently installed by the proprietors of the hotel, separates the neatly-ordered gardens from the chaotic wilderness of the dene, much as the original boundary once separated Frances Anne and her life of incredible wealth and privilege from the dirty, desperate lives of her employees who laboured in her mines and docks a mile or so away. An abandoned, overgrown carriage bridge constructed of shining white-grey stone spans the dene, a long-forgotten connection between these very disparate worlds, its ornate red brick paving just visible here and there under the mud and gravel and weeds.

I trudged through the muddy stream that meanders through the bottom of the dene, past the small cave which was once used in the Hall's heyday to store ice for its distinguished occupants and their guests. The cave is currently lived in by some hardy gentleman of the road – whether by choice or by force of circumstance I do not know – but it is difficult to imagine a more placid spot. Clambering back up the steep ivy-clad banks, I rejoined the footpath which skirts the churchyard and eventually opens out onto Church Lane.

I lifted the latch on the heavy wooden gate and began to walk up the footpath which leads through the churchyard and around to the front of the honey-coloured stone church. I had planned to start my search at the far side of the graveyard, next to the ancient stone wall boundary, under the shade of a large sycamore tree, which stands opposite the church door. There are no regimented rows of gravestones, no neatly clipped lawns or borders; the grass grows long as if in a meadow, rippling in the sea breeze, punctuated with wild flowers. The ancient headstones seem scattered at random, like seeds cast down by a divine hand. For some reason, I stepped off the path into the long grass to my left and turned to face the church, intending to examine every detail of the fabric of this most precious little building. I looked back up towards the small tower and noticed immediately that the flag of St George was missing. Unusual. It's always there, whatever the weather. I glanced down, intending to retrace my steps to the path, and there it was, the very thing I was seeking, right next to the path, the inscription on the golden headstone written on the reverse side, indicating that the occupants of this grave were buried facing the sea.

In Loving Memory of JOHN KNOX
Beloved Husband of ELIZA JANE KNOX
Who Died Sept 28th, 1905 Aged 72 years
Also, the Above ELIZA JANE KNOX
Who died Dec 6th, 1908 Aged 82 years
Also, JOHN aged 17 years
And DAVID aged 14 years
Sons of the Above Who Were Killed
By the Explosion at Seaham Colliery
Sept 8th, 1880

At twenty past two in the morning of Wednesday 8th September 1880, a massive underground explosion tore through Seaham Colliery. So great was the explosion that it was said to have been heard by sailors on ships moored at Seaham Harbour, and by the villagers at Murton, another colliery village a couple of miles inland. Perhaps Sarah Marshall and her employers, Thomas Boland and his wife Jane, were disturbed in their beds at the farmhouse in Seaton; perhaps a few doors down Eliza Knox awoke with a start and knot of dread in her stomach.

At the time of the explosion, the colliery employed some fifteen hundred men and boys and produced half a million tons of coal a year, all of it mined by hand with picks and chisels, by coal hewers crawling on their bellies often in tunnels little higher than their knees, illuminated only by the light from their lamps, stripped down to the waist due to the intense heat. The coal seams and the tunnels which followed their course stretched out for miles underground, even out beyond the coast and under the seabed. Two thousand tons of coal would be brought to the surface of the mine every single day. At the time of the explosion, there were two hundred and thirty-one men and boys underground on the overnight shift, and hundreds of pit ponies. It is believed that more men were working overnight than usual, as some had requested time off to attend a local flower show the next day and were "working up" their hours, or had swapped shifts with their mates.

Such was the force of the explosion that both shafts were blocked, rendering initial rescue attempts impossible. It was at least twelve hours before sufficient debris could be cleared to allow access to the upper seams, and even then, only by lowering rescuers in the kibble, a large basket on a rope, as the cage and winding gear had been destroyed. Nineteen survivors were brought up from the Low Pit shaft; a further forty-eight were eventually brought out alive from the High Pit. As time passed, the hopes of finding any other men alive quickly began to fade.

News of the explosion spread rapidly far and wide. A telegram was sent from the Government Inspector of Mines to the Home Secretary:

> *"I regret to report an explosion of gas at Seaham Colliery at 2 o'clock this morning. Two hundred men in the pit. Shafts blocked. Seventeen men saved in an upper seam. Sounds from men below. Plenty of assistance. Work progressing favourably. Hope to get down before night."*

The Times reported on 9th September 1880, the day after the explosion:

> *"A disaster which appears to be of appalling magnitude occurred at Seaham Colliery, Durham, the property of the Marquis of Londonderry... Women who may be widowed and children who may be fatherless are waiting drearily in the roadways leading to the colliery."* [9]

The Marquis himself was in residence at Seaham Hall at the time, and to his credit was very quickly on the scene. The Home Secretary, Lord Harcourt, visited, and Queen Victoria sent a telegram.

It soon became clear that there would be no more men rescued. Fires still raged everywhere underground and those

---

9   *The Times*, 9th September 1880, dmm.org.uk

parts of the mine that were accessible were too dangerous to enter due the presence of gas and the risk of further explosions. On 10th September 1880, *The Times* described the scene:

> "*The wreckage is fearful. The horses and ponies employed in the mine, about 250, are dead. They have either been killed in the explosion or suffocated.*"[10]

At least four of the horsekeepers, men like Thomas Marshall, Sarah's father, were killed with their ponies, including John Nelson, William Stanton, William Breeze, and John Vickers. On 2nd October, it was reported that a fire had been found in the area of the stables, which was still burning some twenty-three days after the original explosion:

> "*There have now been 100 dead ponies drawn from the pit. One of the horsekeepers, named Vickers, was sent to bank last night. His body was found under a fall. When got out it was so dreadfully mutilated that there was no possibility of recognising him, and his son could only identify him by his trousers.*"

There were heavy losses among the young pony drivers too. David and John Knox, Sarah's young neighbours, were amongst the dead. Their death certificates show that their deaths were not registered until 11th October 1880, some thirty-three days after the explosion, suggesting that their bodies were not recovered for some time, or that they were not easily identified, or both. The certificates were both signed by their mother Eliza with a simple "x" as she was unable to read or write. One cannot comprehend the agony that she and the boy's father went through as they waited at the pithead for news of their beloved boys, their youngest children, eventually burying the boys together in the simple grave in the ancient churchyard at St Mary's.

---

10   Ibid, 10th September 1880, dmm.org.uk

The Knox family were not alone in their grief. There was barely a family in the village left unscathed by the disaster, barely a street that did not lose at least one man. One hundred and sixty-four men and boys perished, along with one hundred and eighty-one ponies – almost eleven per cent of the mine's entire workforce killed in this single incident. The testimony of the rescuers who gave evidence at the subsequent inquest at the Mill Inn bears witness to the horrors they endured, the charred and horribly mutilated bodies they encountered. Families lost fathers and sons, brothers and cousins. Dozens of funerals took place every day, most at Christ Church, which was situated right opposite the colliery and where the memorial to those who perished still stands.

Tales of tragedy and miraculous escapes abounded – one man, Thomas Johnson, had survived all five explosions at the mine. Another man missed his shift because he had overslept, another still had come up to the surface minutes before the explosion because he felt unwell. No doubt the bereaved relatives would have hoped that their loved ones perished instantly and without suffering. However, there is heart-breaking evidence that this was not the case, with some groups of men, unharmed by the initial explosion but trapped by rock falls, surviving in pockets of the mine a thousand feet or more below ground for at least twenty-four hours until overcome by gas or slowly suffocating in the darkness as first their lanterns, and then their air supply eventually ran out.

When more of the bodies were eventually discovered, inscriptions were found chalked on planks of wood next to where these poor desperate souls lay.

"Five o'clock and we have been praying to God."
"The Lord has been with us, we are all ready for heaven –
Ric Cole, 1/2 past 2 o'clock Thursday."

(Written a full twenty-four hours after the explosion.)

There then appears a fainter message, in the same hand:

"Bless the Lord we have had a jolly prayer meeting, every man ready for glory. Praise the Lord – R. Cole" [11]

Perhaps one of the most tragic stories was that of thirty-three-year-old Michael Smith and his sick little boy, young Michael, who died at home on the same day. He scratched a final note to his wife Margaret and three children onto his tin water bottle:

"Dear Margaret,
There was 40 of us altogether at 7am. Some was singing hymns but my thoughts were on my little Michael that him and I would meet in heaven at the same time. Oh, Dear wife, God save you and the children, and pray. Be sure and learn the children to pray for me. Oh, what an awful position we are in!"
– Michael Smith, 54 Henry Street. [12]

Such stories touched the hearts of the nation, and various relief funds were set up to assist the hundred and seven widows, two aged mothers and two hundred and fifty-nine orphans left behind. Donations poured in from around the country. The Londonderrys themselves made personal contributions – the Marquis gave £200, the Marchioness £50, Viscount Castlereagh £50, and Viscountess Castlereagh £25. Queen Victoria sent a gift of £100. A gentleman by the name of Joseph Sebago, of Hyde Park, London, wrote a letter to the Editor of *The Times* on 7th October 1880, enclosing a cheque in the sum of five pounds for the widow of Michael Smith:

"As a director of a large industrial concern in South Wales, I am not altogether unacquainted with miners, and it is

---

11   *Troubled Seams*, John McCutcheon, 1955 DRO DC/ALM 4/10 p. 127.
12   Ibid p. 131.

pleasant to know that, notwithstanding the influence of trade unionism and drink, there are to be found among them such men as Smith."[13]

The Canon of York Minster, Canon Fleming, mentioned the incident in his sermon just a few days after the disaster, using it as an example in his campaign to call for better health and safety for the nation's labouring classes:

"We are compelled to admit that the present means to preserve human life, whether in our mines or on our railways, are entirely inadequate ... much has no doubt been done in the past, but much more remains to be done."[14]

Within weeks of the disaster, relations between the miners and the colliery management began to deteriorate. At the beginning of October 1880, the decision was made, as had happened nine years before following the 1871 explosion, to brick up or "stop" the Maudlin seam in an attempt to allow the underground fires to burn out and so that coal production could resume. This caused outrage amongst the workforce and great distress among the bereaved, as many of the bodies of the victims had still not been recovered. In fact, the last of the bodies, the remains by then mummified, would not be recovered until 6th September 1881, almost exactly a year after the explosion occurred. The *Durham Chronicle* records how a strike was called, but the men went back to work not long afterwards as they were promised increased wages by the colliery managers, and that the Maudlin "stoppings" would soon be withdrawn. Although pay was increased, the managers reneged on their promise to take down the stoppings and remove the remaining bodies. The entire workforce came out on strike in December 1880, in protest

13   *The Times,* 7th October 1880, dmm.org.uk
14   dmm.org.uk

at management's treatment of the widows and their failure to retrieve their fallen colleagues. The widows of those who had perished were each paid one shilling per week, and three pence for the education of each child, but this was paid directly to the school. These funds were paid not by the colliery owner, but from the relief fund. Eliza Knox was paid the sum of £12 in compensation for the death of each of her sons. A group of ten widows famously interrupted a meeting of the relief committee, demanding two shillings and nine pence a week each, and a shilling each for their children. Their requests were refused. Because all of the miners' cottages in Seaham were owned by the Londonderry estate, and exclusively for occupation by employees of the mine, those widows left without a husband or son working at the pit were eventually required to leave their homes or face eviction.

By February 1881, the striking miners were desperate, and the resolve of some began to waiver. A few broke away and returned to work as blackleg (i.e. strike-breaking) labour; blacklegs were also brought in from other mines in the county. The strikers were blacklisted, which prevented them from seeking work at other collieries, and many were threatened with eviction. Disturbances, protests and violence followed, with some of the strike-breakers and the blackleg labour being assaulted by their former colleagues. The Londonderrys came down hard on their upstart employees – fifty men were arrested, including George, Thomas and Simeon Vickers, relatives of the horsekeeper who had perished, John Vickers. Simeon was sentenced to five months' imprisonment in Durham Gaol along with four of his colleagues; a compromise was eventually reached and eight men were victimised. These eight, known as the sacrificed men, were sacked from their jobs and forcibly evicted, with their wives and children, from their homes.[15] They were prevented from seeking work elsewhere.

---

15   *Troubled Seams*, John McCutcheon,1955 DRO DC/ALM 4/10 pp. 116–123.

The Miners' Union awarded each of the sacrificed men the princely sum of fifty pounds to enable them to try to make a new start elsewhere. Some of the men chose to emigrate to America, settling in the coal fields of Pennsylvania. Others followed in their wake, including two of the Vickers brothers, although they did eventually return to Seaham a few years later. Perhaps Sarah Marshall and Eliza Knox were amongst the crowds who gathered at the tiny station at Seaton to show solidarity with the men being carted off by train to prison in Durham; fearful of another riot, the police took the prisoners via a different route. A vote was held amongst the remaining striking miners on returning to work; the majority voted to stay out but they were unable to return the two-thirds majority required and by March 1881 the strike was over.

The inquest proceedings rumbled on, a report was presented to Parliament and a formal Enquiry commenced at the Londonderry Institute in Tempest Road on the 10th October 1880. The Enquiry heard that ventilation in the mine was by means of a furnace fire at the bottom of the shaft. This practice was subsequently made illegal but not for another thirty years. The Enquiry eventually determined that the cause of the explosion had been "shot firing" in the curve between the two shafts, which had probably ignited a lethal combination of gas and coal dust. Incredibly, all four previous explosions had occurred at the same spot and in almost identical circumstances.

Astonishingly, and counter to the direction of the Coroner himself and the huge amount of evidence which suggested gross negligence on the part of the colliery owners, the jury returned an open verdict. Perhaps the jury men, having witnessed the fate of the striking miners, were too fearful of the Londonderrys and their all-encompassing power over the lives of their employees and the village tradesmen to lay any blame at their door.[16] In the longer term, the events at Seaham led to

16   Ibid p. 94.

further research on the explosive qualities of coal dust, which saved countless lives.

For the residents of Seaham and Seaton Village the autumn and winter of 1880/1881 were dark, desperate days. For Sarah Marshall and her family, things were about to get even worse.

6

A Twist of Fate

No matter how carefully we plot our desired future course, no matter how methodically we map out our hopes and dreams, so often fate intervenes. This intervention can take myriad forms. A chance meeting may cause us to fall hopelessly in love with someone entirely inappropriate, someone who may turn our lives upside down, yet cause us to see the world and ourselves in a completely different way for the rest of our days. A single conversation with a passing acquaintance may result in an unexpected but welcome opportunity to change our career and the entire direction of our lives.

But fate is not always kind. The sudden loss of a loved one or dear friend can destroy an entire way of life in the blink of an eye. The safe, the secure, the familiar may disappear in an instant, never to be replaced but never to be forgotten. So it was for the widows and orphans of Seaham and Seaton. So it was to be for Sarah Marshall.

Life for the inhabitants of these small villages went on, though forever changed. Coal production at Seaham Colliery resumed and was soon back to pre-disaster levels. New workers gradually replaced the dead and the injured – there was always some needy soul with mouths to feed willing to step into a dead man's shoes. Miners were recruited from further afield, Scotland, Yorkshire, Wales, Ireland, Somerset, Kent and even Cornwall. Anyone going about their business amongst the colliery village's streets in the 1880s would have encountered a plethora of different accents and dialects. Despite – or perhaps even because of – the suffering of its citizens, Seaham was thriving. Expansion and development continued apace, fuelled by the ever-increasing national demand for coal in Victorian Britain. New municipal buildings, shops, homes and places of worship continued to spring up around the Harbour, including a new Co-Operative store in Castlereagh Road. The trade directories of the time paint a picture of a bustling little town, which catered for its populace's every need and want. There were bakers and brewers, blacksmiths and dressmakers; chemists and confectioners; fishermen, greengrocers, hairdressers, photographers, ship's chandlers and sailmakers.

The town was even home to the French, Swedish, Norwegian, Hanoverian, Russian and Danish Consuls. The docks were teeming with ships of all sizes and nationalities, bringing goods in and taking coal out, and ferrying passengers and workers between the various ports of the north-east coast. Other industries prospered, including shipbuilding just near the Featherbed Rock, slightly north of the Harbour, rope works, gasworks, and the famous bottle works of industrialist and politician, John Candlish.

Candlish, born in 1815 and the son of a Northumberland farmer, was quite a character. He pursued numerous business ventures with varying success, including newspaper publishing, shipbuilding, coal exporting and the gas industry. However, it is for his famous bottle and glass works that he is now remembered. In the early 1850s he took over the Seaham Bottle Works; the business enjoyed the favour of the Londonderrys and was renamed the Londonderry Bottle works and would expand to become, for a time at least, the largest bottle works in the whole of Europe. Up to 20,000 hand-blown bottles and glass receptacles were produced every single day. Seaham glass bottles were exported the world over and the bottle works continued to churn out glass until 1921. Candlish is remembered in street names in Sunderland and Seaham – there is still a Candlish Terrace in Seaham, and still a Bottleworks Road.

If you walk along Seaham beach as the tide goes out, revealing barnacle-encrusted rocks draped with seaweed and glittering rock pools, you will spot folk shuffling slowly, eyes fixed on the sand beneath their feet, hands grasping plastic bags, occasionally bending to pick through the shingle, searching for sea glass. Once the waste products of John Candlish's Bottleworks, these precious pebbles of turquoise, emerald green, opal white, medicine-bottle blue and occasionally citron and ruby are now prized and exported to jewellery makers and craftsmen the world over. On holiday in Maine in 2011, I stumbled upon a little art gallery and craft shop in Bar Harbor, which had on display necklaces and bracelets all crafted from Seaham sea glass. As children we would pick up these pretty nuggets, play with them a while then cast them aside without a thought. In those days, the beaches were littered with them; today sea glass is much more difficult to find. Almost a century after production at his Seaham factory ceased, Candlish's glass is still sought after, though perhaps not in the form he intended.

By the time of the 1881 census, when Sarah Marshall was living in Seaton Village, the population of Seaham Harbour had grown to over seven thousand; New Seaham, the cluster of streets around the colliery was home to some three thousand souls, with a further one hundred and ninety-six in Seaton Village and one hundred and eighteen in Dalton-le-Dale. Sarah Marshall's family had grown too. By now the horsekeeper, Thomas Marshall, and his wife Margaret had six daughters, the youngest, named Margaret after her mother, just four years old. Such was the life of a domestic servant, however, it is very unlikely that Sarah would have seen her family often, maybe once a month or so but possibly less frequently; in all likelihood, she would barely have known her much younger siblings. She had probably gone "into service" at around age fourteen, some five years before the time she was recorded as living in the household of Thomas and Jane Boland at Seaton Village Farmhouse.

Thomas Marshall and his family were then living in Page Bank, a tiny colliery hamlet to the west of Durham city, between the grand house of the Shaftos at Whitworth Hall, and the rambling fourteenth century castle at Brancepeth. It is some thirteen miles or so from Seaton Village as the crow flies. Perhaps Sarah occasionally took a train from Seaton station to Durham, then another the short distance to Brancepeth, and then walked the remaining two and half miles to Page Bank – it's very unlikely that such a return journey could have been easily accomplished in an afternoon. It is much more likely that Sarah kept in touch with her family by letter, with the occasional visit home. We know from her Brisbane emigration records that she could read and write, as could her mother Margaret. Compulsory primary education had been introduced in England in 1870 and although Thomas Marshall and his family moved around County Durham from colliery to colliery during Sarah's childhood, she would have had a rudimentary education at the very least, and would have been one of the first of her generation to benefit.

The life of a young female domestic servant was an incredibly hard one, by any standards. It is difficult for us to imagine a life which involved household chores from the very moment of waking to the very moment of falling asleep, exhausted and bone-weary, with little or no free time other than perhaps a Sunday afternoon off once or twice a month. We do not know whether Mrs Boland was a fair and kind mistress. We do not know how well Sarah and the farmhands were treated. There is little doubt, however, that Sarah's day would have been long, full and back-breaking. Sarah was the only domestic servant employed in the Boland household at that time, and would therefore have been a "maid-of-all-work", the lowest of the low. The Victorian writer Mrs Isabella Beeton described the lot of the maid-of-all-work in her famous work *The Book of Household Management*, published in 1861:

> *"The general servant or maid-of-all-work is perhaps the only one of her class deserving of commiseration. Her life is a solitary one and in some places her work was never done. She is also subject to rougher treatment than either the house or kitchen maid."*

Perhaps the most telling account of the life of the maid-of-all-work appears in the 1858–1859 edition of *The Dictionary of Daily Wants*:

> *"A domestic servant, who undertakes the whole duties of a household without assistance; her duties comprising those of cook, housemaid, nursery maid, and various other offices, according to the exigencies of the establishment. The situation is one which is usually regarded as the hardest worked and worst paid of any branch of domestic servitude; it is, therefore, usually filled by inexperienced servants, or females who are so circumstanced that they are only desirous of securing a home, and of earning sufficient to keep themselves decently clad. In many of these situations, a servant may be very comfortably circumstanced, especially if it be a limited family of regular habits, and where there is a disposition to treat the servant with kindness and consideration."*

This tome goes on to describe how a maid-of-all-work could expect to rise by half past six in the morning at the very latest. She would be expected to first light the kitchen fire, and put the kettle on the range to boil; then she should sweep, dust, and prepare the room ready for the family to have breakfast. After cooking and serving the breakfast, the maid would strip and remake the beds, empty the chamber pots, and clean the bedrooms, before going back to the kitchen to wash up the breakfast things and prepare and cook the lunch.

Once lunch is over and done with, "she is at liberty to attend to her own personal appearance, to wash and dress herself." The afternoon could be spent blacking the kitchen range, perhaps keeping an eye on the Boland children, doing the family sewing and mending, preparing the vegetables for the evening meal, or perhaps Mrs Boland would send Sarah down into Seaham to purchase necessities and run errands. One wonders if whilst shopping and gossiping with the other domestic servants in Church Street Sarah ever bumped into Robert Threadkell, the man who would become her future brother-in-law, before walking the two miles back up to Seaton Village.

In addition to these domestic chores it is of course likely that Sarah, being a servant in a farmhouse, was expected to help out on the farm, perhaps feeding the hens in the yard and chasing them out of the kitchen, gathering the eggs, working in the fields at harvest time, filling the water troughs, assisting with the milking and fetching water from the pump. Carrying water was an endless and back-breaking task, even worse on a Monday, the traditional washing day, when the family clothes and sheets and table linen had to be washed and scrubbed by hand, rinsed, put through the mangle and then hung out to dry, ready to be aired, ironed, folded and put away on a Tuesday. Every day, every week, followed a regimented pattern, hard and monotonous labour interspersed with the occasional light relief of a trip down to Seaham Harbour or a rare visit home to see loved ones. Every night Sarah would climb the steep back stairs next to the pantry to the tiny servant's bedroom overlooking the farmyard, the railway track and the fields beyond.

It is hardly surprising that given the unhappy state of affairs that prevailed in Seaton and Seaham in the early years of the 1880s, the political and social unrest which followed the explosion at Seaham Colliery, and the drudgery of her every day existence that a change began to take place in Sarah Marshall.

The spark of an idea, the seed of a dream – how many of us wish for a different life? We look back with regret on the what-might-have-beens, ponder the infinite future possibilities and yet are unwilling or unable to take that first precarious step into the unknown, to take control of our own lives and change our futures. How often do we simply drift along, grudgingly accepting the status quo because our heads tell us to be sensible, yet all the while our hearts yearn for something more? The hours turn to days, the days turn to weeks, the weeks turn to years and before we know it our lives are almost over, a catalogue of missed opportunities, dashed hopes and faded dreams.

For the vast majority of poor servants like Sarah, whom polite society considered to be the dregs of humanity, there was only one way out of domestic servitude, and that was marriage – frequently to the first young (or not so young) man who came along, swapping one form of drudgery for another. Sarah Marshall, it transpired, had different ideas.

It is impossible to know precisely when the idea of making a new life on the far side of the world first occurred to Sarah, but the stories of two people, one from her past, and one from her present, undoubtedly captured her imagination and she began to conceive of the possibility of a monumental adventure.

In 1879, in his late thirties, Sarah's uncle, Mark Thornton, (her mother's younger brother) had left behind the coal mines of East Durham for a new life in the gold fields of America, settling in the city of Grass Valley, Nevada, with his wife, also called Sarah. They had married as teenagers but had no surviving children. Quite why he chose Grass Valley is unclear, as the gold mining boom was already at an end when he arrived there. Perhaps the Thorntons ended up there accidentally, washed along on the tide of circumstance, as they moved wherever they could find work. In the United States Federal census of 1880, Mark Thornton is described as a labourer. In the 1910 census, he was still there in Grass Valley, aged seventy one, living on Union Hill Road – the stark description, *"emigrated 1879, no children"*, the story of two lives, summed up in four simple words. Mark Thornton never came back to England, and never saw his sister Margaret, or Sarah and his other nieces, again. His occasional letters back home would no doubt have been the subject of intense family discussion, and perhaps provided Sarah with her first imaginings of a wider world, far beyond the village green of Seaton and the pits of County Durham.

A couple of doors down from the farmhouse, the widowed shoemaker, Bryan Hodgson, lived with his three unmarried daughters, Hannah, Eleanor and Jane. There was nothing particularly remarkable about the family, except at the time of the 1881 census, Mr Hodgson also had living with him his daughter – yet another Sarah – and his son-in-law, the magnificently-titled Rector of the Parish of St Thomas, St Kitts, Bahamas, Thaddeus Augustine Constantine Armbrister, and their two young children, Percy and Irene. According to the census records, Percy and Irene had been born in St Kitts in 1875 and 1878 respectively. Quite how the daughter of a shoemaker living in a tiny village near the Durham coast ended up in St Kitts, married to the son of colonial landed gentry and plantation owners was initially something of a mystery. Thaddeus had been born in the West Indies in 1837; his family were plantation owners on Cat Island in the Bahamas. It seems that the family had some sort of connection with North-East England – another of the Armbrister children, Beryl, who had been born in St Kitts in 1873, was recorded as living in Earsdon in Northumberland in the 1881 census, presumably with relatives. The Armbristers' descendants retained close links with the Church though – their great-grandson Ray is the current churchwarden of St Mary the Virgin, once the parish church of Seaton Village and the final resting place of the young Knox brothers, killed in the pit explosion. I spoke to Ray, and he explained that Thaddeus had been sent to England by his parents in the Bahamas to study for the Church; upon completing his studies, he was offered the position of curate at Christ Church in Seaham. Whilst serving as curate, Thaddeus had met and married Sarah Hodgson, and took her back to St Kitts with him on their wedding day, when he took up his appointment as rector of St Thomas. The family returned to Seaham on several occasions to visit Sarah's family, and came back to live in Seaton Village in 1891, shortly before Thaddeus passed away.

Seaton was (and still is) a close-knit community – no doubt Sarah Marshall chatted to Mrs Armbrister during her visits, perhaps as they hung out their washing on the village green, listening to her stories of a far-off island, her tales of life in the Colonies and on board the sailing ships that plied the trade routes from England, across the Atlantic Ocean to the islands of the West Indies. Perhaps the adventures of the Armbrister family, in particular Sarah Armbrister herself, captured Sarah's imagination and she began to dream of the possibilities of making a new life for herself in the Colonies – maybe in America, like her Uncle Mark, maybe in Canada or South Africa. Or maybe even in Australia.

Day dreams are all very well, but the events of 1882 would seal the fate of the horsekeeper Thomas Marshall and his family and act as a catalyst, forcing his daughter Sarah into making the hardest decision of her life.

8th March 1882 saw the birth of another child to the Marshalls, their seventh daughter, Fanny Hood Marshall. Thomas was still working at Page Bank Colliery (also known as South Brancepeth Colliery) when Fanny was born, as a cartman, his days as a horsekeeper now over. We cannot know how the birth of Fanny was greeted – was it a joyous event? Was her arrival tinged with disappointment at the birth of yet another daughter instead of a much longed-for son? Did her parents secretly despair at the thought of having yet another mouth to feed? Sarah and the next eldest girl, Ann, were of course both already "in service", but the Marshalls still had five small daughters to care for. It is likely that both Sarah and Ann would have sent home a proportion of their meagre wages. Their circumstances were not of course unusual, with the average family at that time having five children, but there is no doubt that their lives were a constant struggle.

In early June 1882, just three months after Fanny's birth, Thomas Marshall began to feel unwell, suffering from a urinary infection. Being the hardened colliery man that he was, no doubt he passed it off as a minor complaint and continued to work, in increasing pain and discomfort. However, Thomas began to grow feverish and had to take to his bed – a real worry for Margaret and the children as this would have meant Thomas' wages were stopped. Margaret sent word to Sarah and Ann, summoning them home to see their father, who by the third week in June had become gravely ill. What constitutes a minor illness today, easily resolved with a short course of antibiotics, was to prove Thomas Marshall's undoing. The infection spread, and septicaemia set in.

Observing the change in the face and demeanour of a hard-working man as his days grow fewer is exquisitely painful. First comes the bravado, the fighting spirit, the "Don't worry lass, I'll be alright"; slowly the spirit begins to diminish, gradually giving way initially to acceptance and then ultimately to a longing for the end to come. The fleshy, rosy cheeks gradually sink and grow paler by the day, until they become hollows, features pinched and skin tight, the colour of travertine stone; the eyes that once danced and sparkled now staring, distant and dimmed, the lips which bestowed kisses and laughter and stories in equal measure, now silent apart from occasional delirious murmurings, the name of a loved one the only comprehensible word. His hands, once so strong, skilful and scarred, now barely able to grasp the comforting hand of a wife or daughter. And so, we watch and we wait, we wait and we watch, selfishly hoping against all hope and reason that he will stay with us a while longer – another week, another day, another minute, yet praying for his suffering to end and his soul to be set free.

By dusk on 28th June 1882, at the age of forty-eight, Thomas Marshall was dead.

7

The Long Goodbye

Like the widows and orphans of the victims of the Seaham mining disaster, Margaret Marshall and her five little girls were evicted from their colliery cottage within weeks of Thomas' death. It is difficult to imagine the depths of their despair, widowed, fatherless, and destitute, with no income. There is no record of what happened to them in the immediate aftermath of their bereavement but, as was so common in those days, it is likely that the family was dispersed and the children taken in by various friends and relatives in order to avoid the horrors of the workhouse – the ultimate shame and the last resort of the Victorian poor and homeless.

Elizabeth, the third daughter, who was thirteen at the time of Thomas' death, probably went into domestic service like her two older sisters. Within four years, the second daughter, Ann, had married James Hudson, a Sunderland miner, and by 1891 Margaret and Fanny, then nine years old but a baby when Thomas died, were living with Ann and James and their children at Grindon Cottage, Bishop Wearmouth, on the outskirts of Sunderland, perhaps five miles or so from Seaham. Fanny would always stay close to the Hudsons. In Edie's box of photographs and letters, there are numerous portraits of her Hudson cousins, particularly Jane, known as Jenny, and Amelia, of whom she and her mother Fanny were very fond.

There is no way of knowing when Sarah finally made her decision to start a new life, alone, on the far side of the world.

Was she afraid? Did she question her own motives? How could she leave her poor widowed mother and her six younger sisters? Was she torn or did she possess a steely determination and a clarity of purpose, underpinned by utter desperation and an ambition to achieve bigger and better things? Perhaps her mother begged her not to go; perhaps she pleaded with her not to stay. Margaret must have known that she would never see her first-born daughter again but maybe she considered migration to be Sarah's only chance to escape the dirt, the cold, and the grinding poverty of the family's hand-to-mouth existence.

Why did Sarah choose to go to Australia, and why in particular to Queensland? I pondered this question for some time. Why didn't she choose America, like several other Seaham residents? Sarah's descendants in Brisbane, the Balkins and the Campbells, could shed no light on the matter. However, a clue was revealed in the ship's passenger list and her Brisbane immigration records. These show that Sarah Marshall was travelling as a "remittance passenger". In other words, her voyage was paid for and sponsored by someone else.

My immediate thought was that perhaps Sarah had met and fallen in love with a young gentleman who had travelled to Australia to make his fortune, and when established, had sent for her to be his wife. Perhaps she had answered one of those "wife wanted" advertisements, so beloved of Victorian fiction. However, I could find no evidence of this – one would have anticipated a wedding to have taken place fairly quickly after her arrival, but no nuptials occurred.

I then wondered whether Sarah had gone to join another relative, who, upon learning of the death of her father and the family's straitened circumstances, had offered her a position in the family business or had secured employment for her with an acquaintance. Again, I could find no trace of any other of the Marshalls or Thorntons having emigrated (by choice or otherwise) to Australia. Only Sarah's uncle Mark had left England, for America.

Queensland had achieved separation from the colony of New South Wales in 1859, and formed its own legislative assembly in the same year. However, at that time the new state had a population of just twenty five thousand, not much more than the current population of Seaham, spread across an area roughly seven times the size of Great Britain, five times the size of Japan and two and a half times the size of Texas. Queensland needed infrastructure, it needed people and it needed money, fast.[17] The Queensland government therefore embarked upon an intensive immigration programme almost immediately. From the outset, however, immigration was tightly controlled, and the government made it quite clear that despite the best attempts of the British to clear out their workhouses, asylums and prisons and ship their inmates to the colonies, such "unsuitable" candidates would not be welcome.[18] Queensland required hard working skilled people to "civilise" and tame the thousands of square miles of territory, not the poor, the infirm, felons and the destitute.

Back home, immigration was considered by many to be the last resort, due to its longstanding association with the transportation of convicts, which had ceased in 1868; however, the enterprising Victorians of the 1850s and 1860s began to see it as an opportunity for self-improvement, and the chance to seek a fortune. The first convicts had been sent out from England in 1788; Moreton Bay, in Southern Queensland, near where the city of Brisbane now stands, was originally a penal colony for twice-convicted criminals, but was opened up after the penal colony closed down, so that anyone was free to settle there.[19] In the 1850s, Queensland had no paved roads, no railways and no method of communication with the outside world apart from a very patchy and infrequent mail service. The building of the

17 *Rights of Passage–Emigration to Australia in the Nineteenth Century*, HR Woolcock (Tavistock Publications Ltd), London 1986, p. xiv.
18 Ibid p. 35.
19 Ibid p. 6.

first railway, from Ipswich to Grandchester, didn't even start until 1861 and didn't open until 1865. The few immigrants who did arrive tended to settle in and around Brisbane, and it was difficult to persuade newcomers to move further up the country, and in particular to the tropical far north of the state.

Rather than focusing on and recruiting the wealthy middle classes, members of the professions such as doctors and lawyers, engineers and dentists, gentlemen farmers and those with a private income, the Queensland politicians wanted to recruit the state's new populace from farm labourers, loggers, railway workers, shepherds, and female domestic servants – in effect the government were importing an entire "working class". Queensland needed people who, in the language beloved of modern recruitment consultants, could "hit the ground running". What was needed were tough, industrious people, used to hardship, with the skills to overcome whatever difficulties they might encounter. The role of the female domestic servant was crucial – there was a huge demand for their skills, but they were also needed to redress the imbalance in the male/female population, and ultimately, to breed and increase. If it was to succeed, Queensland needed to be populated.

Of course, Queensland already had an indigenous population who had lived there for thousands of years. In a pattern replicated throughout Australia, and indeed in so many other colonies of the British Empire, the indigenous population were shamefully and brutally treated by the incoming pioneers, and in many areas, simply wiped out. HR Woolcock writes in *Rights of Passage*,

> *"Aborigines were either ignored or exterminated. The colony, despite its climate and location, was to be a white man's land with immigration directed towards introducing a suitable European, and predominantly British, population."*[20]

20   Ibid p. 11.

The journey itself was enough to deter many would-be immigrants. It's a daunting trip now, even though it can be accomplished in a little over twenty-four hours; in the 1850s and 1860s, immigrants faced a two or three month journey by sea. The horrors of the transatlantic migrant ships, particularly those that left Ireland for New York during the famine, were well documented in the newspapers and literature of the day. The dreadful insanitary conditions, overcrowding, terrible sea-sickness, on-board epidemics of diseases such as diarrhoea, cholera and measles, combined with badly-equipped and ill-maintained ships and poorly-trained crews resulted in high mortality rates, particularly amongst children. Tales abounded of immigrant parents burying their children at sea, one after another, as they made their way to the New World.

The Queensland government knew that, in order to attract the calibre of people the state needed to develop and expand the population, they would have to greatly improve the "immigrant experience" –and this started with the journey. Back in Britain, Parliament had already passed The Passenger Act of 1855 which imposed minimum standards on immigrant ships. Representatives of the Queensland government were dispatched to London and embarked upon a huge PR campaign; the law makers in Brisbane put in place a raft of legislation designed to control every aspect of immigration, from imposing standards on shipping companies to ensure the safe deliverance of their precious cargo in a fit and healthy state, to organising grants of land to those who landed ashore, in order that they could build homes, farm the land and provide for themselves. A deal was signed with the Black Ball Shipping Line to provide ships ferrying immigrants from London and Glasgow, and taking goods and mail back to Britain on the return journey.

The arrangement with the Black Ball Line quickly went awry, however; the shipping owners agreed to provide free passage to any immigrant who agreed to sign over his land grant to the company, but in return they insisted on being allowed to carry a proportion of fare-paying passengers without any of the usual selection criteria imposed by the Queensland government. This resulted in land grants being swallowed up by the Black Ball owners, and the swathes of land which would have been colonised, farmed or otherwise developed stood vacant. In addition, many of the fare-paying passengers turned out to be completely unsuitable and lacking in the skills required to "make a go of it". The Black Ball ships were not run as they should have been; terrible conditions on board and high death rates on some of their ships ultimately resulted in the government contract being terminated.

A financial crisis in Britain in 1866, followed by economic woes and unemployment in the fledgling state meant that the Queensland government still struggled to attract the "right sort" of immigrant. However, everything changed when gold was found in Queensland in the early 1870s, and people flocked there in their thousands from Europe and from elsewhere in Australia. The good days didn't last long – a corruption scandal in the Queensland government immigration office in London in 1875 coincided with economic depression in the state, part of the seemingly endless cycle of "boom and bust" that would plague the colony well into the twentieth century and which would have heart-rending implications for some of the other people we will meet in this story.

In 1880, the Queensland parliament introduced new immigration rules designed to root out any weaknesses and corruption in the old system, and signed an exclusive contract with the newly-formed British India Steam Navigation Company.[21] The age of sail was coming to an end. The government launched yet another recruitment campaign, focusing on experienced agricultural workers and female domestic servants. Sarah Marshall was one of those to benefit from a "perfect storm" for the would-be Australian female immigrant – new technology resulting in faster journey times and better conditions on board

21   Ibid p. 19.

ship; a more direct route to Australasia as a consequence of the newly-built Suez Canal; and a huge demand for experienced female domestic servants. For Sarah and women like her, there was never a better time to go.

Prior to researching Sarah's story, I had never heard of the Single Female Migrant recruitment programme. Between 1850 and 1890, one hundred thousand single British women and girls emigrated to Australia, recruited, and passage paid for, by the colonial governments. Some forty-six thousand women were given free passage by the State of Queensland; twenty thousand of those left London and Glasgow in the 1880s alone, due to a desperate shortage of female domestic servants to service the burgeoning middle-class population of Brisbane, Cairns and beyond.[22] A fair portion of those women and girls were from the north east of England – Northumberland and County Durham.

According to leading academic Jan Gothard in her book, *Blue China – Single Female Migration to Australia*,[23] almost four times as many working-class women emigrated to colonial Australia as were sent out on the convict ships. The offer of free passage meant that very poor women like Sarah Marshall did not have to scrimp and save to scrape together their fare from their meagre wages – this in itself made Australia a more attractive proposition to the poorest emigrants than, say, America or Canada. The fact that there was a shortage of domestic help meant that, upon arrival, employment was virtually guaranteed. Rather than being considered the dregs of humanity in British society, the female domestic servant seemed, on the face of it at least, to be valued and sought after in the Colonies.

But how would Sarah have learned about Queensland and the promise of a new life there? As part of the recruitment programme, the colonial government established a network of agents and publicists throughout Britain and Ireland. These

---

22 *Blue China – Single Female Migration to Australia*, Jan Gothard
    (Melbourne University Press) 2001, p. 6.
23 Ibid pp. 30–38.

agents toured the country giving lectures in churches, village halls, sporting clubs, workers' associations, and at fairs and festivals.[24] Advertisements were published in both national and local newspapers, in journals and periodicals, and posters appeared in every town and city. Of course, the more people who migrated, the more information about life in Australia made its way home to their friends and relatives. Migration was nothing new – many County Durham miners had sought out new lives abroad in the aftermath of industrial unrest, and this was even reflected in the street names of the colliery village of New Seaham, with pitmen and their families occupying cottages in California and Australia Streets. There is even a Seaham in New South Wales, not too far from Newcastle.

Due to the Queensland government's stringent criteria for their recruitment programme, acceptance was by no means guaranteed. There was a rigorous and lengthy application process. Sarah would have first completed an application form, with details of age, occupation and providing the names and addresses of three referees, including her local religious minister, her doctor and her most recent employer. Perhaps Mrs Boland and the Reverend Thaddeus Armbrister provided references. All references were always followed up, with particular attention paid to checking that an applicant was of good "moral character and sober habits". Any young woman with an illegitimate child, a criminal conviction, a fondness for strong drink or a "colourful past" would not be considered. A poor reference from an employer could ruin a would-be migrant's plans. Likewise, any health problems, past or present, would automatically have ruled her out.

Jan Gothard describes in *Blue China* how moral fibre was given equal weight alongside domestic skills, experience and physical condition. Emigrating domestic servants were looked upon as a commodity, as precious cargo. Soiled goods were not wanted. A young woman would be expected to conduct herself

24   Ibid pp.30–38.

with the utmost integrity both before departure, during the voyage and upon arrival in the colony, and strict measures were put in place to ensure that she did not stray from the path of righteousness at any time during the process.

To modern eyes, the Victorian obsession with morality appears very old-fashioned, however, it underpinned the Single Migrant Recruitment programme for two very good reasons. Firstly, these young women from the lowest strata of British society would be welcomed into the middle class homes and families of complete strangers in Queensland, and had to be completely trustworthy. Secondly, they had to be "wife and mother material" to fulfil their subsidiary role of increasing the population of the colony. Fortunately, in the opinion of the agents of the government of Queensland, Sarah Marshall appears to have been well thought of by those who provided her references. She possessed the "right stuff" and she was accepted onto the programme in 1886 as a remittance passenger, her fare paid for by the state.

The winter of 1886 was a particularly harsh one. Snowdrifts six and seven feet deep were reported on the roads of Seaham and Seaton Village. On a bitterly cold morning in late October 1886, Sarah said her goodbyes to her widowed mother and younger sisters and boarded the train at Durham station, bound first for London. Even in the 1880s, London could be reached easily in the course of a day by steam-train. The view from Durham station remains one of the most magnificent from any station in England. Did she look back from the station high above the city, one last glance down over the ancient jumble of medieval, Georgian and Victorian rooftops to the towering Cathedral and princely Norman castle keep beyond?

Every one of us has stood on the brink, hearts leaping and leading us forwards, ready to step off the precipice of the routine, the everyday, the familiar, yet 'reason', the rope tangled around our hopes and ambitions pulls ever tighter, restraining, choking and eventually suffocating our dreams.

How many times have we paused, waiting at the gates of something new, something life-changing, the gates that will open up to reveal the path to our heart's desire, only to prevaricate too long? We watch, helpless, as the gates slowly begin to close, the weight of old loves and old lives, old ties and old lies eventually slamming them shut forever.

Would you have been strong enough? Would I? Do we have the strength of character, the determination, the single-mindedness to seize the day, to grasp opportunity with both hands, to struggle out from beneath the weight of familial expectation and the crushing need to be seen to "do the right thing"? Are we sufficiently resolute to escape one future and exchange it for another? Several times in my life I have wavered, and failed to take that leap. I wasn't bold enough. But Sarah Marshall was.

Sarah would not see the beautiful city of Durham, her village home, the mining folk of Seaton and Seaham, nor her family, ever again.

8

Precious Cargo

On the morning of 1st November 1886, Sarah Marshall stepped on board the steamship, the *SS Duke of Sutherland*, at Gravesend on the Thames Estuary, having taken the train from the newly-opened Immigrants' Home in Blackwell, London. Sarah would have been required to arrive at the Home, which was basically a lodging house run along the same lines as a ship, two or three days prior to embarkation, in order to be issued with her kit for the journey, have her luggage inspected, and to undergo further rigorous checks regarding her suitability. How daunting this must have been for any passenger, let alone a young woman travelling alone from the colliery villages of County Durham. Sarah Marshall, however, was no ordinary woman. How did she feel as she walked up the gangway, dragging her few possessions behind her? Hesitant? Nervous? Excited about what lay ahead tempered with relief at finally escaping her old existence? Or fear, bordering on terror, that she was making the biggest mistake of her life? I suspect a combination of all.

As a remittance passenger, funded by the Queensland government, Sarah's "ship's kit" would have been paid for. The kit, issued to all but first class passengers, included essentials for the voyage such as a bedding roll, sheets, water bottle, a dish for washing in, a plate, a mug, cutlery and large amounts of soap.[25]

---

25 *Rights of Passage – Emigration to Australia in the Nineteenth Century*, HR Woolcock (Tavistock Publications Ltd), London 1986, p. 99.

Passengers were allowed twenty cubic feet of luggage. This sounds a lot but in reality, amounted to no more than a couple of small trunks. Sarah was allowed to keep with her only one item of luggage containing items and spare clothing necessary for the journey, as space in the berths between decks was extremely limited. The rest of her possessions were placed in the hold until arrival at her final destination.

In addition to luggage checks, Sarah had to submit to further medical examinations by two doctors, one of whom was the ship's surgeon, Dr Poland. The Surgeon Administrator, as well as being the ship's doctor, was second only to the captain and was responsible for all administrative matters on board ship, as well as the health and welfare of the passengers. Unusually, Dr Poland's wife was also travelling, which suggests that perhaps they were not intending to make the return journey. Dr Poland was assisted in his enormous task by Mrs Turnbull, the matron. The role of matron was a very wide one, covering everything from attending to all of the medical needs of the single female passengers to organising entertainments and concerts for the children on board. Her principle goal, however, was to prevent any "fraternisation" between the men on board (including the crew) and the single ladies. The crew were completely forbidden from communicating with the passengers – any attempt to do so could result in instant dismissal.

The SS *Duke of Sutherland* was unlike anything Sarah would have seen before, and would have dwarfed the colliers' merchant vessels and fishing boats which docked at Seaham Harbour. The *Duke* had been built by Duncan & Co in Glasgow in 1873 for the Eastern Steamship Co (Ducal Line) which traded between the UK and India. A massive three thousand and thirteen gross ton iron steamship, she had a maximum speed of eleven knots and was around three times the size of the average emigrant sailing ships which had preceded her. The Queensland government had signed a new contract with the British India Steam Navigation Co in 1880, and in 1884 an agreement was made between the

Ducal Line and BISN Co for Ducal Line ships to trade alongside the former's ships on the Queensland migrant route. The *Duke* could accommodate sixty first-class passengers, together with a vast number of migrants – around eight hundred in total – who were housed in bunk compartments between the decks. In practice, passenger numbers usually hovered around the five hundred mark. She remained in service on this route until 1902, some sixteen years after taking Sarah to Brisbane.

Steam ships had many advantages over sail – as well as their enormous capacity, they were generally safer, were very fast, were not dependent on the winds and tides, were reliable (provided they were maintained well) and could therefore be chartered to provide very regular services to transport people, goods and mail between Great Britain and the rest of the Empire. The use of sails on these types of commercial journeys more or less disappeared by the turn of the century. Steam power cut the journey time to Australia by a whopping fifty per cent. What steam ships did require, however, was vast amounts of good quality coal. As a result, the major shipping lines established coaling ports at regular distances along the main routes. Although steam was much quicker and more reliable than sail, it was incredibly dirty and also created extremes of temperature on board. Deaths due to heatstroke among passengers multiplied after the steamers were introduced, and became the most common cause of death amongst adult passengers – those unfortunate enough to have their quarters close to the engine room particularly suffered. Passage through the Suez Canal and the Red Sea, always the hottest part of the voyage, could see temperatures on board hover around a hundred degrees Fahrenheit night and day.

Mortality on board migrant ships remained of constant concern to the colonial governments. Steam ships, whilst not without the risks associated with high temperatures, were by and large not troubled by the major outbreaks of disease which had plagued the sailing ships transporting first convicts and then migrants to both Australia and America. Death rates among passengers travelling across the Atlantic to New York at the height of the Irish Famine in the 1840s and 1850s averaged ten per cent; on some ships, it was as high as forty per cent. Just forty years later, around ninety nine per cent of passengers travelling on board a steam ship to Queensland could expect to complete the journey; most fatalities on board were amongst children who succumbed to diseases like measles and pneumonia. The improvements in death rates can be attributed to a number of factors, not least the shorter journey times, rigorous health checks at the port of embarkation, the presence of an on-board surgeon and matron on every trip, a constant supply of fresh water from condensers and the introduction of refrigeration which meant that live animals no longer had to be carried and slaughtered on board.

Mortality rates on the many German migrant ships headed for Australia were significantly higher – these ships tended to be much less regulated and more overcrowded; the continental migrants, as they were known, were not subject to the rigorous pre-departure health checks faced by British migrants. The highest number of deaths recorded on an Australian migrant ship was seventy seven, on the German-registered *Sultana*, after an horrendous one hundred and fifteen days at sea; all but two of the dead were children. Surprisingly, even death rates on board the convict ships were less than two per cent, but perhaps this can be explained by the fact that most of the passengers would have been young men, and very few children, the most vulnerable to heat and disease, would have been on board.

The greatest risks to steamship passengers (apart from heatstroke) were from accidents and collisions, running aground on reefs and rocks, and shipping water in heavy seas. Even the largest, sturdiest-built ship would have been thrown around like a cork in very bad weather. Given the huge number of journeys the migrant ships made to Australia (some figures estimate as many as one thousand three hundred and seventeen voyages were made), only three ships were ever lost. The last was the *SS Dacca* which sank with all hands in the Red Sea in 1890. Incredibly, it wasn't until 1888 that it became law for all ships carrying migrants to be fitted with life-saving equipment.

The *Duke of Sutherland* was involved in her fair share of incidents at sea; in September 1902, she struck a reef off Lizard Island in the Coral Sea and was stranded for six days without any means of contacting the outside world.[26] Several unsuccessful attempts were made to reach Cooktown in Northern Queensland but it wasn't until a week later that they managed to communicate with a small passing steamer which bore news of their predicament to the mainland. Eventually she was refloated and limped to Cooktown for repairs. A newspaper report from the *Sydney Morning Herald* of 3rd October 1902, describes (with an understatedness bordering on the hilarious) how the *SS Duke of Sutherland* passed Cairns "leaking only slightly". A passenger by the name of Hugill recounted how *"the vessel appeared to have ploughed her way through the top of a coral reef … the passengers took things quite philosophically and made quite a picnic affair."*

A very strict daily regime was imposed on board all emigrant ships to ensure that order was kept at all times and also to guarantee the cleanliness and therefore health of the ship and her passengers. Sarah slept in an iron bunk in a small compartment with five other girls. Passengers were expected to be up and about by seven in the morning before attending to their ablutions, dressing, rolling up their bedding, sweeping around and under their bunks and cleaning the whole accommodation area. Breakfast was between eight and nine o'clock, lunch at one o'clock, supper at six in the evening, and "lights out" was at ten o'clock.[27] Passengers were divided up into groups of between ten and twelve, known as a "mess", along military lines, for the purposes of daily cleaning duties and cooking. The surgeon

---

26 *Sydney Morning Herald*, 3ʳᵈ October 1902, trove.nla.gov.au
27 *Rights of Passage*, HR Woolcock (Tavistock Publications Ltd) London 1986 p. 101.

appointed a group of constables from among the senior male passengers, to keep watch during the night and to ensure that order on board was maintained. In effect, this meant keeping an eye on the single female quarters just in case any amorous young gentleman on board was tempted to pay a late-night visit.

Dr Poland would also have selected a teacher for the children on board, who were required to attend classed for six hours each weekday. The older children and young adults were encouraged to attend evening classes, while educational lectures on a wide variety of topics, including life in Queensland and what immigrants could expect upon arrival, were organised for the benefit of the other passengers.

To modern eyes this may appear a fairly grim and tedious routine, however, Sarah would have found that after the completion of her cleaning and cooking chores she had a great deal of leisure time on her hands. For a former maid-of-all-work, this would have been something of a novelty, and for Sarah the voyage would have been the one and only time in her life that she ever experienced anything approaching a "holiday".

To fill in the long hours, passengers would organise deck games and sports like cricket were played frequently, although anyone scoring a six was very unpopular for obvious reasons. Sarah and her female companions organised concerts and dances, put on plays, and held parties for the children. There was an extensive library on board – the ship's records show that a very high proportion of the passengers were literate. On Sundays, the surgeon issued the children with sweets and birthday parties with extra treats were a regular feature. Additional rations were provided at Christmas. Many of the poorest passengers on board experienced a standard of living and a quantity of food they could only dream of back home. Throughout the activity programme the proprieties were always observed, and the single ladies were kept separated from the men at all times. Alcohol was completely banned, even for the first class cabin passengers, and only Dr Poland had access to a small supply, literally for "medicinal purposes".

Incredibly, there exists in the annals of the *Brisbane Courier*, an account of the *SS Duke of Sutherland's* journey from London to Brisbane precisely one year after Sarah's departure.[28] This voyage was almost identical to Sarah's as the ship called at the same ports and even sailed under the same captain and crew. This report of the journey – a moment paused in time – provides a wonderful description of what everyday life on board would have been like for Sarah and her fellow passengers and the hazards they would have encountered on the way.

Wednesday 4th January 1888 – The Brisbane Courier.

THE DUKE OF SUTHERLAND

The B.I.S.N. Company's supplementary steamer Duke of Sutherland, 2024 tons, Captain J. S. Cox, from London, via ports, with immigrants and a general cargo, anchored in the Brisbane roadstead at midday yesterday and was assisted up the river on the afternoon's tide by the tug Beaver, berthing alongside Messrs. Gibbs, Bright, and Co.'s wharf, Kangaroo Point, about 3 o'clock. The Brisbane contingent of her immigrants, to the number of 295, having been duly inspected by the immigration agent, were landed on the wharf, and marched from there to the new immigration depot, Kangaroo Point, where they were comfortably housed. Their luggage was transhipped into lighters, and will be landed at the old depot in William Street, as there is no accommodation yet for it at the new premises.

The Duke left London with a total of 485 souls, equal to 427½ statute adults, who were placed under the charge of Dr. Marshall as surgeon-superintendent, and Miss Wale as matron. Nationalities: 204 English, 69 Scotch, 201 Irish, and 9 from other countries.

---

28   *Brisbane Courier*, 4th January 1888, trove.nla.gov.au

Classification: 39 free, of whom 21 are English, 4 Scotch, and 14 Irish; 405 remittances and free nominated passengers—152 English, 63 Scotch, 182 Irish, and 8 from other countries; and 39 full payers. The assisted, free, and remittance and free nominated passengers paid a total of £400 towards their passages and ship's kits.

Occupations: 132 female domestic servants, 109 farm labourers, 45 general labourers, 1 gardener, 11 miners, 1 blacksmith, 1 bricklayer, 1 carpenter and joiner, 1 wheelwright, and 10 others whose trade or occupation is not specified. Social condition: 51 married couples, 166 single men, 156 single women, 43 males and 44 female children between the ages of 1 and 12 years, and 12 infants. The Duke of Sutherland landed 1 single male and 4 single females at Thursday Island; at Cooktown—5 single males and 5 single females; at Townsville—6 married couples, 28 single males, 28 single females, and 18 children; at Rockhampton—2 married couples, 12 single males, 13 single females, and 4 children; at Maryborough—6 married couples, 12 single males, 15 single females, and 16 children; leaving 18 married couples, 106 single males, 91 single females, and 62 children for Brisbane.

The Duke of Sutherland, which, as already stated, is under the command of Captain Cox, left the Royal Albert Docks at 1.30 p.m. on Friday, the 4th November.

The following particulars concerning the voyage have been kindly furnished by Mr. H. Lyndamore, her popular purser. The Duke anchored off Gravesend at 5.20 p.m. on the 4th November for the night, and embarked the emigrants at 1p.m. on the following day. The anchor was weighed at 11.30 p.m. that date, and Gibraltar was passed on the 12th. She passed Malta on the 17th, but did not call on account of the prevalence of cholera there; arrived at Port Said at 3.30 p.m. on the 18th; left same date and reached Suez on the 21st, leaving again same date.

On the 26th of that month a fatal casualty occurred. An able seaman, named Wylie, by some means fell overboard, and, although, the vessel was stopped for two hours, he was never seen again. Colombo was made on the 6th December, and left on the 7th, and she arrived at Batavia on the 15th, leaving again on the same date. On the 17th of that month, when passing through Lambok Straits, the vessel was caught in a tide rip, and shipped large volumes of water both fore and aft, which caused no small amount of alarm amongst her passengers.

She reached Thursday Island on the 24th of December, and left on Christmas morning. A slight accident occurred as she was leaving this port. In swinging round preparatory to leaving, the Duke of Sutherland, owing to the strong current running at the time, fouled the hulk Star of Peace, which is stationed there. The result was that her after gig was smashed.

She arrived at Cooktown on the 27th, left that afternoon, and anchored in Cleveland Bay on the 28th; left at 11.30 p.m. on the 30th; arrived in Keppel Bay on the 31st, and off the White Cliffs, Hervey Bay, on the 1st instant; left on the morning of the 2nd, and, as before stated, anchored in the Brisbane roadstead at midday yesterday.

The Duke experienced fine pleasant weather all the way to Townsville, but from that port to Maryborough she had to contend against strong head winds and squally weather. The general health of the immigrants during the whole voyage has been excellent, and there has not been a single death. There was one birth when the vessel had reached Hervey Bay. The immigrants are a strong and healthy-looking class of people, and have proved amenable to discipline during the entire passage. Their quarters have been kept scrupulously clean, which no doubt accounts to a very great extent for the entire freedom from sickness. The monotony of the voyage was agreeably relieved by concerts, which were held regularly twice a week, and which were always numerously attended. Altogether the voyage of the Duke of Sutherland has been a very pleasant one. The vessel will be reported at the Customs this morning, and discharging operations will be commenced forthwith."

The unfortunate man overboard, Wylie, had in fact met a gruesome end. Captain Cox described in the official report of his death, *"It is believed that when the third mate saw Wylie throw up his arms, that he was then pulled down by a shark for he was never seen to rise again."*[29] The description of a voyage during which one crew member was eaten by a shark, and during which the ship nearly sank, as a "very pleasant one" is I think testament both to the general acceptance of the perils of seafaring in the 19th century and the stoicism of the emigrants.

On Sarah's voyage, the *Duke's* four hundred and ninety nine passengers were mainly young fit working class people in their twenties and thirties; as well as the young ladies travelling under the Single Female Migrant scheme, there were a number of single men, but also married couples travelling with children. Groups of older siblings were not uncommon – the young Humphreys brothers, Edwin (23), Alfred (21) and young William (16), all travelled together, as did the Wyeth family, consisting of twenty-four-year-old Mary Ann Wyeth and her four younger brothers, the youngest of whom was only fourteen. As I poured over the passenger list, I pondered the fate of each of these young people and wondered what life in the colonies had held for them.

The route that the old convict and immigrant sailing ships took to Australia was incredibly circuitous. Totally dependent

---

29 *Rights of Passage*, HR Woolcock 1986, ibid p. 176 (Crew List BT 99/1568).

upon the winds and currents, a typical immigrant ship would sail down the Thames to Gravesend before heading round into the English Channel and the Bay of Biscay, then making for the Atlantic Ocean. Instead of heading south and following the west coast of Africa, the ship would sail south-west towards South America. Upon reaching the South Atlantic, the captain would hope to pick up the winds to take his ship back across the southern-most reaches of the Atlantic and veer east towards South Africa and around the cape of Good Hope. These ships were so far south that foul weather was virtually guaranteed. Passengers could expect to encounter snow storms, raging seas, huge waves and even icebergs. The captain would eventually begin to plot a northerly course, passing Tasmania before heading up the coast of New South Wales and then to Queensland. Incredibly, no stops were made en route unless there was some sort of emergency on board and the ship had to put into port for repairs. Passengers could be on board without sight of land for three months. Voyages in excess of one hundred and twenty one days were recorded – an unimaginable seventeen weeks at sea.

The opening of the Suez Canal in 1869 changed everything and revolutionised the transport of people and goods between Europe, Asia and Australasia, cutting thousands of miles and up to several weeks off the journey to Queensland. This incredible feat of engineering which had taken ten years to complete, combined with the use of the new steam-powered ships, reduced the voyage time to around sixty days, although one ship managed to complete the distance in just forty five. An emigrant ship could now travel through the Mediterranean to the Suez Canal, pass through the canal from Port Said to Suez, sometimes stopping at both ends of the canal to take on coal, then sail down the Red Sea to the Port of Aden where it would make another stop before heading out into the Indian Ocean and around the southern tip of India. The ship would put into port in Colombo in what was then Ceylon (now Sri Lanka) then east to Batavia (Jakarta) in

Indonesia where a final coal stop would be made. Queensland waters would finally be reached just west of Thursday Island, the northern-most point of Australia.[30] The ship then had to negotiate myriad small islands (including Lizard Island, where the *Duke* was destined to run aground in 1902) and the Great Barrier Reef as it hugged the coast of Queensland, dropping off cargo and passengers at various small port towns along the way to Brisbane, its final destination.

I had wondered what Sarah would have made of the sights, sounds and smells of these exotic foreign ports, places far beyond her experience or imagining. Sadly, I learned that she would have seen very little of them; usually only the fare-paying passengers were allowed onshore when the ship was in port. It's unlikely she'd have got to see much more than the docks at any stopping-place on the voyage. I found this somewhat strange. Were the migrants considered too untrustworthy to be allowed off the ship? However, it is to be remembered that Sarah and her fellow passengers were precious cargo – the Queensland government, who was funding their voyage, did not want their investments to be corrupted in any way, either physically by disease (or more likely, by alcohol) or morally.

Foreign sea ports were no places for single young women travelling alone, whatever their social status. The shipping lines contracted to the government were paid a premium for each live passenger landed in Australia, and they were not prepared to lose anyone on the way. If any outbreaks of disease were reported in the forward ports, none of the passengers at all would be allowed to disembark, and only those crew members essential to the unloading of cargo and the loading of coal were permitted on dry land. On the *Duke's* previous journey, one gentleman who had been taken ill had been left behind in a hospital in Colombo.

Incredibly, I have been able to follow every day of Sarah's voyage using old shipping reports and telegrams sent by

30   Ibid p. 78.

71

shipping agents to the owners and local newspapers upon the *Duke's* arrival at each port.

The *Duke of Sutherland* sailed from Gravesend on the afternoon of 1st November 1886. Her arrival in Port Said exactly two weeks later, on the 15th November, was reported in the Sydney Evening News. She reached Suez within a further two days, and appears have to sailed straight on to Colombo arriving on 2nd December. After taking on coal and provisions, she made her way briskly to Batavia in Indonesia – the Newcastle *Morning Herald* reports her departure on the 13th December "*for the Queensland Ports*". Sarah's first sight of Australia was of Thursday Island on around 17th December, as the *Duke* passed through the Torres Straits, bearing south east.

The *Duke's* first port of call in Queensland was Cooktown, in the far north, where the ship remained in harbour for two days, and where the first of the immigrants disembarked on 21st December. Sarah celebrated Christmas Day on board the *Duke* attending a brief carol service and having a special Christmas Dinner with the other young women. The *Duke's* progress was not halted by the festivities however, with more passengers and cargo being delivered to Townsville, and the small settlements of Bowen and Mackay. Keppel Bay and Port Alma near Rockhampton were reached on Boxing Day, Sunday 26th December.

A large number of passengers had disembarked in Townsville and Rockhampton, including Maurice and Barbara Jones and their five-year-old son Moffatt – tragically their baby boy had died on the voyage and been buried at sea. Baby Jones was one of four babies under the age of twelve months to perish on the journey. The others were all baby boys too – George Morgan, Jesse Wright and Henry Barker. The eight baby girls and two other baby boys on board all survived. The causes of the infants' deaths are not noted on the ship's passenger list – the simple words "Died on the voyage" are written in pencil alongside each of their names. Despite the advances in sanitation and technology, a two month sea voyage was still fraught with risks for the very young, although of course infant mortality rates generally were much higher in the 1880s, whether at sea or on land. Any passenger who perished on the voyage, whether a baby, an older child or an adult, would be wrapped in sail cloth or cotton sacking and, after a prayer and a few words said by the Captain, consigned to the deep.

The *Duke of Sutherland* arrived in Hervey Bay on 27th December, with passengers and two locomotives to be delivered to Maryborough. Progress was delayed somewhat when, during the unloading process, the crane lifting one of the locomotive boilers toppled over and the boiler crashed onto the deck. Fortunately, no one was injured. The ship was further delayed at Maryborough and the passengers were not allowed to disembark as there was no doctor available to inspect the ship for quarantine purposes. The nearest doctor, Dr O'Connor, had to be fetched from fifty miles away and was somewhat disgruntled by the experience, according to reports in the Maryborough Chronicle on Wednesday 29th December. Eventually, after a two day delay, the thirty-one immigrants were given a clean bill of health and were brought ashore by the paddle steamer *Pacific*.

In the early morning summer sunshine of 30th December 1886, the *Duke of Sutherland* steamed into Moreton Bay. Sarah Marshall rolled up her mattress for the last time, put on her second-best dress, tidied her hair and climbed the steps up to the main deck.

Brisbane.

9

Brave New World

Sarah was in for a shock. Whatever she was expecting, whatever she had dreamed of, there's a fair chance that the Brisbane of December 1886 fell a long way short. After disembarking with their luggage, Sarah and the other girls were shepherded to the overcrowded and shabby immigration depot at William Street for "processing" (the new immigration depot at Kangaroo Point would not open until December 1887). There they would have remained, possibly for a few days, billeted in the packed dormitories with dozens of other new arrivals, whilst their papers were processed and employment secured, anxious, apprehensive and perhaps even frightened.

The city itself was a building site, a seething mass of humanity which would see its population more than double from a little around thirty-seven thousand in 1881 to over ninety thousand just ten years later, through wave after wave of immigrant arrivals and the drift of rural workers from throughout Queensland and northern New South Wales.[31] The 1880s saw Brisbane's metamorphosis from a frontier town to a sophisticated urban city, a little bit of Victorian England recreated in the Australian sunshine.

Back in 1817, Lord Bathurst had established an enquiry into the transportation of felons to New South Wales – the fear was that the regimes in the existing penal colonies weren't quite severe

---

31 "Occupations of the People of Brisbane: An Aspect of Urban Society in the 1880s", DP Crook, *Journal of Historical Studies: Australia and New Zealand* Vol.10 Iss.37, 1961, www.tandfonline.com

enough, and were doing nothing to deter would-be criminals in England. He sent John Thomas Bigge to investigate; it was decided that new, more isolated, even more grim settlements were required for repeat offenders, and Moreton Bay was chosen as a possible site. Bigge "discovered" a river flowing into the bay, and named it after the then Governor of New South Wales, Sir Thomas Brisbane.

The first settlement was established by the Surveyor General, John Oxley, on 28th September 1824, and is commemorated by a somewhat dull granite obelisk which is arguably in the wrong spot. In typical understated Australian fashion, the inscription simply reads:

"Here John Oxley Landing to Look for Water Discovered
the Site of this City."

Terrible grammar too.

The first convicts followed shortly afterwards, and by the time of the creation of Queensland as a separate state in 1859, the settlement had grown into a town of some six thousand residents. Up until the mid-1860s, Brisbane had been very much a pioneer settlement – there was no sanitation, no drainage, no proper water supply, very few roads, no lighting and no public transport. Water was drawn from fetid swamps and there was a high mortality rate, particularly amongst the under twenty-fives – deaths from malaria and typhus and other waterborne diseases were daily occurrences, a fact of life.

Within just twenty years, the city had expanded exponentially. By the time Sarah arrived, vast improvements had been made to the infrastructure. The first Town Hall was built in 1865, and was followed by drainage and sewage systems and reservoirs to guarantee fresh drinking water. The city was illuminated by gas lighting, and public parks and recreational reserves were created. The first tramway had opened in 1885, and Central Station, which linked Brisbane with other Queensland towns, was completed the same year.

The building boom of the 1880s which created so many of the city's grand public buildings including the Government Printing Office, Customs House, new Town Hall, together with many commercial buildings – warehouses, banks, hotels, theatres, breweries, distilleries, boatyards, foundries, brickyards and engine works – meant that labour was always in demand. It also led to a whole jumble of architectural styles, from neo-classical to Gothic revival and everything in between; columns, porticoes, pillars, arches and "pointy bits" appeared on these very grand buildings, all contributing to a vision of the city as being a bit, well, over the top.

The writer Anthony Trollope visited Brisbane around this time, and described it as:

> "...a commodious town, very prettily situated on the Brisbane River...with Courts of Justice, Houses of Parliament, a governor's residence, public gardens, and all the requirements of a capital for a fine and independent colony."[32]

The novelist Gilbert Parker, arriving in Brisbane in 1889, was less impressed. In his travel journal: *Round the Compass of Australia*, he remarked:

> "Brisbane is in appearance scraggy, low built and premature. It is far from picturesque as a whole, and the first impressions are not changed by closer inspection. There is a sense of disappointment, which grows deeper as the sojourn in the capital is continued. One gets the impression now of a town that is but half-dressed."[33]

---

32 *Australia & New Zealand Vol I* Trollope, A (George Robertson) Melbourne 1873 p41
33 *Round the Compass in Australia* Parker, G (EW Cole) Melbourne 1892 p213

What did Sarah feel? Impressed? Disappointed? Or just overwhelmed by the enormity of her new surroundings? From the late Autumn frosts of a Durham mining village, where every face would have been a familiar one, to the sub-tropical heat and humidity of a Queensland summer and a city where she was completely alone, Brisbane was, for Sarah Marshall, a Brave New World.

Sarah may well have felt alone upon arrival but in fact she was far from it, being one of ten thousand, six hundred and thirty-one emigrants who came ashore in Brisbane in 1886. In today's anti-immigration political climate, the scale of migration to Brisbane is almost impossible to comprehend. A total of seventy-nine thousand, two hundred and fifty-one emigrants entered Brisbane between 1880 and 1890; this figure does not include the thousands who disembarked at the more northerly Queensland ports.[34] The vast majority of these souls were English, Scots and Irish, with smaller numbers of Welsh and German. Then, as now, immigration was a thorny subject, with some of the "established" population objecting to what they saw as an influx of the dregs of British and Irish society – unskilled labour. A chap by the name of Henry Jordan, ironically a former government immigration agent, wrote to his local newspaper:

> "For the last 16 or 17 years we have been expanding enormous sums of money in sweeping together... the poorest of the people of England ... and bringing them out to this colony. I protest at the importation of mere labourers, who come in shiploads, month after month, year after year. To that kind of immigration is to be attributed the larrikinism in our streets."

It wasn't just the "mere labourers" who faced criticism either. In some quarters the young women who poured into the city under the Single Female Migration Scheme were viewed with

---

34 Ibid.

hostility. The *Northern Argus* newspaper featured an article on the 23rd February 1881 which viciously portrayed these young women as harbingers of crime and vice:

> *"...many of whom have shewn directly upon their arrival that they have come direct from the streets; from reformatories, without reformation; or were girls from country towns and villages, who, having made themselves disagreeably conspicuous in some shape or other, were packed off to London to a labor agent...it is not necessary to insist upon what is known to be a fact, namely, that many of our female immigrants become charges upon the public, either by their being compelled to seek assistance from the Benevolent Society, or by becoming inmates of our Hospital or Gaol."*[35]

Although there was always the odd "bad apple" who slipped through the system, and no doubt a few unfortunate women who fell upon hard times on arrival and into prostitution, particularly during 1883 when there was a massive influx of migrants and the supply of workers briefly exceeded demand, these were certainly a very small minority. The opinion expressed in the *Argus* was, quite simply, based upon prejudice and not fact. The Queensland government imposed strict criteria upon the selection of would-be immigrants, and it is very likely that most of those considered "unsuitable" or of "questionable morals" would have been weeded out by the immigration agents back in England.

Fortunately for Sarah, she arrived at the height of the boom years of the 1880s, when the demand for experienced domestic servants was at its peak. The *Daily Observer* newspaper reported in March 1886 how: *"Every servant, good or bad, is snatched up the moment she offers"*, which of course meant that wages were relatively high. General servants could expect to earn a weekly wage of around ten to fifteen shillings, housemaids ten to twelve

---

35 *Northern Argus*, 23rd February 1881, cited in DP Crook, ibid.

shillings, domestic cooks fifteen to eighteen shillings, and cooks in the larger hotels as much as twenty to twenty five shillings.[36] For some reason hotel barmaids were paid particularly well, perhaps because they were hard to come by, it being considered "inappropriate" employment by many young ladies.

Massive population increase in a very short space of time meant a shortage of housing. While Brisbane's elite could afford to build grand villas, the majority of the populace was crammed into simple wooden cottages. Just because a domestic servant could earn a relatively decent wage, she was not guaranteed adequate living accommodation. Generally, she would have "lived in" with the family or provided with quarters if she was employed in a hotel. One well-off lady complained that:

> "Many, very many indeed, of the rooms reserved for servants in this colony are totally unfit to be occupied by any human creature as often as not the servant's room is some outhouse or a room next the stable; I have even known of a girl being put to sleep in the saddle room." [37]

It wasn't just the living conditions that were problematic; the working conditions were appalling, especially for women working in the factories who did the same work as their male counterparts, for incredibly long hours, for a fraction of the pay. In this respect, the working environment differed little from what might have been encountered by workers in the industrial towns and cities back home in England. Unskilled workers were particularly vulnerable, and the horrors of child labour loomed as large in the colony as they did back home in the factories, mines and mills of Victorian Britain. An article in the imaginatively-titled newspaper *The Brisbane Boomerang* in January 1888, described how working conditions for women in the city were deteriorating year after year:

---

36 Ibid p. 13.
37 *Daily Observer*, 9th March 1986, cited ibid p. 44.

"They are becoming herded in stifling workshops and ill-ventilated attics; they are dragged back to work late on summer nights; and they are forced to stand all day behind the counters of the large emporiums that are the boast of great towns. They are 'sweated' by clothing factories and boot factories; they are housed, when servant girls, in disgraceful kennels; they are used in this fair Australian land, well-nigh as badly as they are used in the modern Babylon of Wealth and Want...And the children too are being dragged into the slave-houses of toil; little ones who should be at school, or at play, are working in the factories and shops, and the law, instead of rescuing them...stands by to ply the whip on their backs if they revolt." [38]

The plight of the city's working poor led both to a Government Commission in 1891 (and subsequent legislation to reduce working hours), and a burgeoning labour and trade union movement. Skilled and unskilled workers alike began to organise, campaign and in some cases strike, much as the miners of Seaham Colliery had done ten years before. The bakers of the city, after striking and with widespread public support, managed to negotiate a reduction of their working hours to ten a day (fourteen or even sixteen hour days prior to this was not uncommon). Very slowly, over subsequent decades, conditions for the workers of Brisbane began to improve.

In 1887, Sarah found herself to be one of almost three thousand domestic servants in the city. I wondered what had become of her. Did she find employment straight away? Was she snapped up by some respectable family with a nice home, well treated and well looked after? Or did she end up as a "slavey", the Australian equivalent of the maid-of-all-work, the lowest of the low, working herself into the ground, ten thousand miles from home and wishing she was back there? No record of her employer exists, but after much searching, I managed to find a

38 *Brisbane Boomerang*, 7th January 1888, cited ibid p. 41.

record of Sarah living in Turbot Street, in the commercial heart of Brisbane. Because of this, I believe it is likely that Sarah found work in one of the many hotels which lined that street.

Turbot Street then, as now, is one of the city's main thoroughfares; then, as now, it was lined with business premises and hotels, and was home to Brisbane's market. Farmers from all over Queensland would bring their fruit, vegetables, meat and dairy, to the indoor warehouse market on Roma Street, which ran parallel; their produce would then be set out on the many market stalls on both sides of Turbot Street, ready for sale. The street would have been full of stalls and barrows, market traders calling out to passing customers, ponies and carts, the air heavy with a heady mixture of fruit and horses, as servant girls and housewives moved from stall to stall amongst the hustle and bustle to purchase the provisions for their mistresses or families.

There were other new arrivals on Turbot Street in January 1887 too. At the corner of Turbot and George Street, roughly where the Friendly Society dispensary building stands, there appeared an establishment by the name of Higgins' Menagerie. This was a small, private, travelling zoo which took up residence in Brisbane, much to both the consternation and fascination of the city's residents. This was no small collection of half-domesticated farm animals and pets. Higgins' Menagerie boasted African lions, Bengal tigers, assorted monkeys, snakes and other exotic animals.[39] These unfortunate creatures were kept caged and chained for the amusement of passers-by in what are described in local newspapers of the time as *"ramshackle, dangerous and stinking premises"*. Sarah must have walked past the Menagerie every day on her way to the market, perhaps pausing to look at the forlorn animals and chatting to their tormentors.

The tigers, however, had the last laugh. Or rather, the last bite.

---

39   This account of Higgins Menagerie and the man-eating tiger appears in a web article from The McWhirters' Project, 22nd March 2013, www. themcwhirtersproject.com, and is based upon a news report of the day.

During a busy lunchtime on Wednesday 21st October 1888, the residents of George and Turbot Streets were somewhat alarmed when one of the menagerie assistants, a chap by the name of Peter Bertram, came hurtling out of an alleyway, covered in blood and screaming, hotly pursued by Sammy, a full grown male Bengal tiger. Sammy had mauled the unfortunate Bertram in his cage. The local newspaper describes how Bertram, trying to escape, had fled the menagerie, unsurprisingly not pausing to close the gate, and Sammy gave chase down Turbot Street. Equally unsurprisingly, Bertram soon discovered that tigers can run faster than people – Sammy, *"his vast frame flying through the air as if propelled from a catapult …felled him to earth with one blow of his terrible paw."* Sammy attacked his victim once again, shaking his body in his jaws like a rag doll. He then dropped poor Bertram, who somehow managed to get up and try to escape, only to be pounced upon and seized a third time by the enthusiastic Sammy. The beast had Bertram completely pinned down, and he was only saved from a grisly end when the proprietor Higgins and the beautifully-named Valentine Spendlove intervened. After turning on his master, Higgins, and taking a fair chunk out of his arm, Sammy eventually got bored, and, *"by the dint of much flogging"*, was finally driven back into the menagerie and chained up again.

Amazingly, all the participants in this sorry episode survived – not least poor Sammy, who miraculously escaped being shot. After much campaigning by citizens and businesses in the immediate vicinity, the menagerie was eventually sold and Higgins and his animals moved back out to Toombul, (where they had originally been bred by Higgins at the Toombul Tiger Farm). The tigers were apparently kept on long chains just two hundred metres from the Toombul Railway Station, pacing up and down, growling and snarling at the terrified passengers.

Brisbane offered many other diversions and entertainments to occupy Sarah in what little leisure time she had available to her. Perhaps she visited the Gaiety Theatre, the Opera House, the Theatre Royal, or maybe the Town Hall which catered more for "working class tastes", with boxing matches and hypnotists. Opera and classical concerts were very popular, and there were regular variety performances at the Oxford Music Hall.[40] There were all sorts of sporting activities available, such as rowing, cricket, cycling, football, rugby, swimming and sailing, though it's not clear to what extent these pastimes were considered suitable for young ladies. Sarah may have had her portrait taken by one of the fifty-two photographers' establishments operating in Brisbane at the time – if she did send any photographs back home to her family in County Durham they have disappeared or been lost or destroyed. In Edie's box, I have photographs of Sarah's sisters, her mother, her brother-in-law and her nieces. Sadly, not a single photograph of Sarah still exists.

In 1887, Queensland was at its zenith. The Brisbane building boom of the 1880s was at its peak, and in rural Queensland the farmers were thriving too. By the end of the decade, the number of sheep in the state had increased from seven to twenty million, and heads of cattle from three to six million.[41] The sugar cane industry was proving lucrative, and new technology in shipping and refrigeration meant that Queensland's meat could be more easily transported around Australia and exported abroad. There was a lot of money to be made by the enterprising, the inventive and the hard-working, and much of that new money was spent in Brisbane. Land in the city became phenomenally expensive, with prices peaking around 1890.

1887 also marked the Golden Jubilee of the accession of Queen Victoria to the throne. Across the British Empire, this momentous event was marked with festivities and civic events, from Canada to New Zealand, and many places in between. Back in Seaham Harbour, school children were issued with

---

40 Occupations of the People of Brisbane: An Aspect of Urban Society in the 1880s, DP Crook, *Journal of Historical Studies: Australia and New Zealand* Vol.10 Iss.37, 1961, www.tandfonline.com

41 Ibid.

commemorative coins, and picnics and concerts were held, together with civic receptions for visiting dignitaries. The Jubilee Methodist Church opened in what is now Eastlea Road, right opposite Seaham Colliery and then at the very edge of the pit yard. New streets sprang up, including Viceroy Street, named in honour of the occasion. Ten thousand miles away in Queensland, Brisbane also marked the 50th anniversary of the Queen's coronation with the creation of a new housing development, the Jubilee Township Estate, out towards Bardon. Plots of land were auctioned off to purchasers wishing to live at such eminent addresses as Empress Terrace, Queen Street and Sceptre Row, and various events took place across the city to honour Her Imperial Majesty. Victorian Brisbane was at the height of its commercial success in 1887, but the spiralling property prices and building boom couldn't last, and by 1890 Queensland and its capital were plunging into a deep depression.

The document I discovered which records Sarah's residence as Turbot Street is dated 7th December 1887. Unfortunately, it doesn't give the name of the establishment where she worked, nor a house number to pinpoint her precise location. There is no clue as to the identity of her employer, nor a specific description of her duties. She is described simply as a "domestic servant". However, it does reveal other intriguing and crucial information about Sarah and her new life in Brisbane.

The document is Sarah Marshall's marriage certificate.

10
Ghinghinda

Sarah's new husband, William John Campbell, was an Irishman and a farmer from Ahoghill near Ballymena, in County Antrim, in what is now Northern Ireland. Ahoghill was and remains a staunchly Protestant area, infamously remembered as the location of the murder of Catholic village chemist shopkeeper William Strathern by Protestant paramilitaries in 1977 at the height of "The Troubles". Like the rest of the island of Ireland, the village and its inhabitants suffered terribly during the potato famine which blighted that country between 1845 and 1852, and which resulted in a massive decline of the population, with an estimated million souls starving to death. Another million departed its shores either voluntarily or by forced evictions by absentee landlords, to start new lives in America, Britain, Canada, South Africa, New Zealand and Australia.

Today, it seems incomprehensible that the British government of the time stood by and watched its Irish subjects starve. Whole generations of families were wiped out, entire villages left deserted.

The guiding principle of British government in the 1840s and 1850s was one of laissez-faire, a doctrine which meant minimal interference in economic affairs. The Irish were left to "get on with it", in the genuine belief that the crisis would "sort itself out". There was a widely-held view that the Irish people were entirely responsible for their own predicament and that they were too stupid to grow crops other than potatoes to feed themselves. They were looked upon by many of the British governing elite as idle, uneducated, ignorant savages, who deserved every misfortune that befell them.

William Campbell was born in Ahoghill in 1844, the second of nine children of farmer Thomas Campbell and Elizabeth Shaw, and was something of a "dark horse". Little is known about his early life – there is simply no record of him anywhere, from after his birth, until his marriage to Sarah. Several of his brothers and sisters emigrated, some to America (via Australia), some to New Zealand. Two of William's younger brothers, Samuel and Hugh, arrived in Adelaide, South Australia, on the *Trevelyan*, in October 1875, but no record of William's arrival exists. According to Campbell family stories, there is a suggestion that William and one of his brothers left Ireland for South Africa, as they were escaping the law. There is no record of William in South Africa, although if he was on the run it is entirely conceivable that he entered that country under a false name. It is rumoured that William then made for Sydney, and found work as a cedar cutter, eventually making his way north to Queensland.[42]

By 1887, William Campbell was living in George Street, Brisbane, just around the corner from Turbot Street. Perhaps the young Englishwoman caught his eye as she made her way amongst the market stalls; perhaps she waited on him in one of the large hotels, pouring his drinks or fetching his supper; perhaps they bumped into each other whilst staring at the lions and tigers in Higgins' Menagerie, where their respective streets crossed. William married Sarah Marshall on 7th December 1887, at the Brisbane Registry Office. William was almost twenty years older than Sarah; his occupation is given as farmer, as is that of his father; Sarah is described as a domestic servant. Her father? "Thomas Marshall (deceased) –Horsekeeper".

Was this a love match or a marriage of convenience? Had William been married before? Had his first wife passed away, or

---

42 I am indebted to Coline Murphy for her research and notes on the Campbell Family History.

perhaps been abandoned? Maybe had he decided to put his wild days behind him and settle down. It is possible that Sarah viewed the union as a means of escape from her life as a servant girl, like so many of her class, perhaps as her younger sister Fanny would when she eventually married Robert Threadkell. It's also possible that she was charmed by this roguish Irish farmer and genuinely in love.

Amongst the faded and fragile sepia photographs in Aunt Edie's box, there is an image of a group of nineteen moustachioed men, dressed smartly in suits, waistcoats, shirts and ties, handkerchiefs in their breast pockets, one row standing, one row seated in front of them, with two young women sitting on the grass at their feet. All are facing the camera, unsmiling, hats removed and hanging on the bushes behind them. Fourth from the left, there stands a tall, slim elderly gentleman, with a balding head, high cheekbones and a bushy white moustache, dignified and proud, though perhaps a little frail. On the back of the photograph, in Topsy Campbell's handwriting, there is the intriguing inscription *"This is a Groupe [sic] of Gov. Inspectors. Your Uncle is the fourth from the left."*

This is the only surviving image of William John Campbell, taken around 1912, when he was about sixty-eight, and the description raises more questions than it answers. I could find no record that he ever worked as an inspector. However, there is no denying the fact that this smart elderly chap must have been a handsome man in his prime.

After their marriage, William and Sarah took lodgings south of the Brisbane River, on Logan Road, in the rapidly expanding district of Woolloongabba, about two miles south of Turbot Street, near to the busy railway yards and the horse tram route and just around the corner from where the famous Gabba cricket ground now stands. Originally an old droving route, once used by farmers to take their livestock to market in Brisbane, by the time the newly-married Campbells moved in at the end of 1887, Logan Road was a busy commercial area with shops, business premises, locomotive works, factories, timber yards, hotels, churches, schools and houses. The suburb of Woolloongabba had for many years been known as One Mile Swamp – up until the mid-1860s it had been just that, and the area was still prone to flooding on a regular basis.

Although William Campbell was described on his marriage certificate (and indeed in all other official documents) as a farmer, given his residence on George Street in the centre of Brisbane just prior to his marriage, and the newly-weds' relocation to the urban district of Woolloongabba, it's unlikely that William was farming at this point in his life. There is no evidence that William actually worked any land of his own when he married Sarah. He had probably moved to the city to find work, perhaps hoping to save sufficient money to purchase his own land. Many men described in official documents as "farmers" worked in the cities or wherever there was well-paid work available, for at least part of the year, particularly during the frequent droughts which blighted the area, or during the floods which laid waste to thousands of square miles of farmland and pasture for months at a time.

Almost exactly a year after the wedding, on 14th December 1888, Sarah gave birth to their first child, a healthy boy, James, at the house in Logan Road. I often wonder how her family back in County Durham must have felt upon receiving news, first of her marriage, and then of the birth of her first son. Happiness yes, but perhaps tinged with sadness and regret that none of them – neither Sarah's mother Margaret, nor her six younger sisters – would ever be likely to see her again. Nor would they ever get to meet her husband and family. Maybe Margaret simply felt relief that Sarah was safe and happy and making a success of her new life, well away from the poverty and straitened circumstances that she and her other daughters had found themselves in since Thomas Marshall's death. It is evident from the letters and photographs in Aunt Edie's box that the two families managed to keep in fairly regular contact, despite the distance, and that there remained a great affection between them.

Aunt Edie's box of treasures. This photograph of Queensland schoolchildren in May 1912 triggered my curiosity.

Seaton Village. Village Farmhouse is the white-gabled building to the right of the Dun Cow public house.

*Margaret Marshall,
Sarah's mother, in 1915.
As a small child I was
convinced she was a
witch*

Edith Threadkell – Aunt Edie.

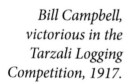

*Bill Campbell,
victorious in the
Tarzali Logging
Competition, 1917.*

Seaham Harbour 1910.

The last pit pony, Darkie, Murton Colliery 1972 (with permission of Murton Heritage Society).

Bill and Topsy with Willie and baby Jean c1914.

Bill, Topsy and 2 of their 6 children, on the porch of their cottage.

*The Campbell's cottage at the foot of
Tamborine Mountain c1914.*

The Campbell farm as it is today.

Bill Campbell (right) 1911, just after his mother's death.

The Gunalda Hotel.

Bill Campbell (left) logging in the Atherton Tablelands, 1936.

John and Lydia Clyde (my great-grandparents) with their children Lydia and Jack c1925.

Looking through the eucalyptus trees from Tamborine Mountain.

Visiting an old friend – Sarah's grave, Upper Coomera.

In 1889, Sarah was settling into her new role as a wife and mother in a respectable working-class suburb of Brisbane, devoting her every waking moment to caring for her new baby and her husband. Life has an annoying habit of being incredibly unpredictable. Just when everything looks rosy, when we are feeling happy and content with our lot, and making plans for the future, events beyond our control can suddenly turn our world upside down. So it was to be for Sarah and William. Towards the end of that year, construction work in Brisbane began to slow down and the need for labour began to decline. By 1890, the city was plunging headlong into the worst economic depression in its short history, as property values crashed and the supply of workers far outstripped demand.

There had been massive speculation, particularly in land sales, by British-based and foreign investors throughout the 1880s. Worried about the gap between actual and promised but ultimately unsustainable returns, these investors began to withdraw their funds. Land and rent values began to tumble. Business and politics were riddled with corruption and nepotism, and as the flow of money into Queensland began first to slow down and then to dry up altogether, public works such as railway and road building were brought to a halt, resulting in soaring unemployment. In the countryside, a simultaneous drop in wool prices resulted in both the sheep station owners and their shearers finding themselves in dire straits.

The *Brisbane Courier* reported that:

> "The foundries of Brisbane are all but deserted; plant which had hitherto kept itself bright has become dust-covered; there have been no ships to build, no sugar machinery to construct, bridge building has been at a dead standstill... timber yards, like foundries, are practically depopulated."

Such was the level of unemployment within the city that a labour bureau was opened, with some two thousand unemployed men registering in the first three months alone. Soup kitchens were established by churches and charities to feed the destitute. Businesses large and small collapsed like dominoes and the economy was decimated. Industrial unrest inevitably followed, with the Great Maritime Strike of 1890, and the infamous Sheep Shearers' Strike of 1891.

By April 1892, it was estimated that as many as twelve per cent of Brisbane's houses stood empty and abandoned. The State government encouraged men to leave the city to look for employment "up country", on the farms and sheep and cattle stations of rural Queensland, and even provided free rail tickets. These often isolated and in some cases desolate spots, sometimes hundreds of miles from the nearest town, were no place to raise families and many men left their wives and children behind. A few never bothered coming back, and their abandoned families were left to survive by whatever means they could.

The sudden and rapid economic decline of 1890 wasn't just a Brisbane problem. The desperate economic situation in the Queensland capital was replicated throughout the state and throughout the country. In Melbourne, sixteen small banks and building societies went under in 1891 alone, and in 1893 the Federal Bank itself collapsed. Thousands of people, of every class and income level, from shipping and railway magnates to shopkeepers and smallholders, lost everything they owned. By May 1893 almost seventy-five per cent of Queensland's banks had closed their doors. Economic turmoil was compounded by natural disasters – in early 1893 huge floods swamped southern Queensland, and Brisbane in particular was severely affected. Countless numbers of livestock were drowned, railway lines and roads were cut off, bridges were swept away, warehouses and goods destroyed, homes and families flooded out.

Australia was on its knees.

In the midst of this chaos, with his dreams of financial security and prosperity in tatters, Sarah's husband William Campbell made a decision that would shape the course of his family's lives forever. Unable to find work in the city, William knew that like many other men of his class, he had no alternative but to leave the little house in Logan Street, cross the Brisbane River and head north or west, to the Darling Downs or even beyond, deep into the heart of the Queensland bush to look for work, perhaps as a farmhand or labourer on one of the sheep or cattle stations which lay scattered across the interior of the State. Unlike those other men however, William couldn't contemplate leaving behind his young wife and their baby James. Torn between financial necessity and grave concern for the welfare of his family, William finally elected upon a course of action which would, indirectly, affect his relationship with Sarah for their rest of their days together.

On a Spring day, late in 1890, Sarah bundled up her baby in her arms, turned the key in the lock of the house on Logan Street for the last time, and walked down the path onto the street, where William was waiting for her, all their belongings and those items of furniture which could be dismantled and reassembled elsewhere, stacked on the back of a hired wagon, protected by a tarpaulin and secured with rope. Once again, Sarah was leaving behind all that was familiar, for another life, unimagined. This time, however, she was not alone. The little Campbell family were headed for Ghinghinda Station.

Ghinghinda is still a remote settlement today. Even with the benefit of paved roads and tarmac highways, it lies over five hundred kilometres northwest of the heart of Brisbane, roughly the same distance from Seaton Village to Stavanger or Brussels. Now in the administrative county of Banana Shire, in 1890, Ghinghinda was still part of the old county of Taroom and was as far away from bustling, cosmopolitan Brisbane as was conceivable. By horse and cart, along dirt tracks and drovers' roads, it would have taken the Campbells at least two weeks travelling to reach the settlement. As they left Brisbane, they passed from town to town, heading towards Toowoomba and out to Jondaryan. Small towns gave way to villages and then to sheep and cattle stations, as the Campbells headed out into the vast, wild, unpopulated expanse of Western Queensland.

Ghinghinda station lies on small plain near the Dawson River, to the west of Kangaroo and Magician Gully and just south of what is now the Theodore State Forest and the Isla Gorge National Park. A photograph of the station taken in 1899 shows a huddle of low, white buildings set in the lee of a small hill, surrounded by a few stunted trees, and set amid scrubland with tree-covered hills in the distance, criss-crossed with creeks that trickled into the Dawson. To the left of the buildings are the stock fences and pens typical of every station in Australia, to the right of the 'big house' occupied by the owner or manager there are a couple of small, squat cottages.

Subject to extremes of climate, temperatures regularly reach thirty-three degrees centigrade in summer, with accompanying thunderstorms, plummeting to as low as six or seven degrees in winter. The land is washed and fed by heavy rains from November to February. It was, and remains a desolate and lonely spot, miles from the nearest homestead or settlement and a lifetime away from the friends and acquaintances Sarah had only just made upon arrival in Brisbane. Of course, an itinerant lifestyle, never staying in one place long enough to put down roots, was nothing new to her; she had spent her childhood travelling between the colliery villages of County Durham as her father moved from pit to pit, year upon year, seeking better pay and conditions.

Ghinghinda could not have been more different. This was no close-knit colliery community. In 1871, twenty years before the Campbells arrived, the Queensland census records that there were only fifteen people living on the entire station. There was no network of assorted female relatives and friends to provide advice, gossip and comfort.

There would have been no more than a handful of women on the station, if any at all – perhaps the station manager's wife, or the wives of some of the more senior station staff, but class distinctions would have meant it was unlikely that Sarah would have socialised with the manager's family. There may have been one or two other families at Ghinghinda at most. Other than that, there was no one. Station life could be a desperately lonely existence for a woman. In the famous collection of tales by Steele Rudd, *On Our Selection*[43] the author describes how his mother would sit on a log and cry every day due to the sheer loneliness of life on their remote Queensland farmstead.

Loneliness, isolation and extremes of climate and landscape weren't the only dangers the pioneers and station families faced. This was Australian life at its harshest extreme – rough living, in a rough landscape, among rough men. A few years before, one of the Ghinghinda station overseers, a man called Salter, had been murdered by a shepherd after a drunken argument. Just forty miles away, one of the most notorious events in Queensland history had occurred in October 1857, the Hornet Bank massacre.[44]

The Fraser family had taken over the running of the Hornet Bank homestead in 1854. Originally from Scotland, John Fraser had moved his entire family – his wife and eleven children, who ranged in age from three years old to early twenties – to this remote farm, miles and miles from civilisation. John died of dysentery a couple of years later and his eldest son William, a particularly vicious individual, took over the running of the farm. Prior to the homesteaders' arrival, the land was occupied by the indigenous Yeeman population who bitterly and often violently opposed the theft of their land by European settlers. The Yeeman were subject to appalling violence by the Fraser clan, which they repaid in kind. Twelve tribesmen were murdered for allegedly killing cattle on the property; there were even rumours that the Frasers had poisoned a group of tribespeople by feeding them a Christmas pudding laced with strychnine.

---

43   *On Our Selection*, Steele Rudd, Bulletin, Sydney, 1899.
44   "From Hornet Bank to Cullin-la-Ringo", Gordon Reid, presented to the Royal Historical Society of Brisbane, 28th May 1981.

At around two o'clock in the morning on 27th October 1857, a group of Yeeman men crept into the Hornet Bank homestead, apparently intending to kidnap one of the Fraser women. When one of the young men on the property confronted them, he was killed outright. The raiders then attacked the other occupants of the house, killing the older males first, before raping and beating to death Mrs Fraser and her two eldest daughters. They clubbed to death the remaining children and then ran through with spears the two station hands who were just returning to the house. One boy miraculously survived, fourteen-year-old Sylvester. He had been beaten around the head, possibly knocked unconscious, but came to and hid under his bed until the slaughter had ceased. This poor traumatised and injured child then ran to the next sheep station at Cardin some twelve miles away to raise the alarm. Sylvester then rode on to Ipswich three hundred and twenty miles away to fetch his elder brother William.

Groups of farmhands from the surrounding stations formed a posse and, in conjunction with the Native Mounted Police, embarked upon indiscriminate killing sprees, murdering any Aboriginals they encountered – men, women and children. William Fraser began a murderous vendetta, killing Aborigines wherever he found them; two were found not guilty of taking part in the massacre following a trial at Rockhampton, but were shot dead by William as they left the court house. At no time was William Fraser ever arrested or charged with murder; in fact, he rode with the Native Police, who were both cognisant of and complicit in the hunting down and murder of the Yeeman. Fraser actually took up a commission with the police a few years later, which allowed him to continue with his campaign of what now would be described as ethnic cleansing. It has been estimated by various sources that between one hundred and fifty and three hundred Aborigines were killed; in any event, the Yeeman tribe was effectively wiped out. It says much about social and political context of the time that Queensland considered William Fraser to be a hero; today he would be considered a mass murderer or a war criminal.

Incidents of violence between the settlers and the local tribespeople gradually petered out over the next few decades, mainly because there were so few of the indigenous population left to protest their cause; some of those that remained were employed by the station owners as scouts and shepherds and labourers. However, the cruel and inhumane treatment of the Aborigines by individuals and government agencies alike was to continue for almost another hundred years.

This was the situation that Sarah now found herself in, an environment far beyond her imagination and comprehension, among people whose way of life she neither knew nor understood. Sarah was clearly a young woman with a steely resolve, unphased by hardship and life's serendipities – like the typical Durham colliery lass she was, she simply rolled up her sleeves, made the best of her situation, and got on with it. However, even she could not be prepared for what the brutal Queensland backcountry had in store for her.

11
The Good Wife

Life for William and Sarah out at Ghinghinda was hard, unrelenting, back-breaking and governed by the vicissitudes of the climate which veered from drought to flood. One can only imagine how Sarah must have felt upon arriving at the family's outback home for the first time. How her heart must have sunk as she entered the rustic dwelling that was to be home for herself, William and their beloved little boy James.

The typical working class accommodation in the Queensland bush was the slab hut, so called as it was constructed from large planks or slabs of whatever wood might be available, with a shingle roof and an earth floor, which was sometimes covered in sand or straw. The roof was usually extended on one side, supported by wooden posts, to provide an overhang for much-needed shade and to ensure that rain ran off away from the wooden sides of the building. Occasionally, the hut might have a tin roof but this would have rendered the dwelling almost uninhabitable in the summer due to the intense heat. Usually divided into two rooms, it was the most basic of dwellings, with no water or sanitation of any kind, and was in reality nothing more than a shack with a fireplace and a chimney. Gaps between the planked walls meant that the hut was usually barely watertight; occupants often covered the walls with layers of newspaper to cover up the spaces and keep out the draughts. In the wet season the hut would have been freezing, damp and potentially ankle deep in mud. Frequently there was no glass for windows, and the window spaces were covered with wooden shutters fastened with pegs. The overcrowded, cramped but solid miners' cottages of West Rainton, Page Bank and Seaham Colliery, with their kitchen ranges, one or two upstairs bedrooms and backyard privies, must have seemed like palaces in comparison to the situation in which Sarah now found herself.

The larger sheep and cattle stations were in effect like small villages, complete with a grand house for the manager, cottages for the senior employees, stable blocks, a large woodshed where the shearing and sorting of the wool took place, pens for the sheep, and washing pools where the sheep were cleaned in readiness for shearing. Sometimes there was a school room, a store selling everything from basic household provisions such as flour and jam to saddles and guns (usually at a significant mark up if there was no competition from storekeepers in the nearby settlements), a blacksmiths shop, a joiner, and sometimes even a small church or chapel.

Some of these stations occupied such enormous swathes of land that it is difficult for modern day readers to comprehend their size. Dunlop Station in New South Wales was one of the largest, at one hundred thousand acres – a single fence on the property was said to stretch forty three miles. The station owners argued that such vast estates were necessary to provide grazing for the huge numbers of animals they supported; some stations were home to hundreds of thousands of sheep. Ghinghinda was tiny in comparison, a mere speck on the landscape, with its small homestead, handful of huts and cottages, and woolshed.

Australian Merino wool was sought after the world over. Allegedly, Merino sheep became popular after King George III had taken a fancy to a few of the animals belonging to the King of Spain; they had been introduced to Australia in the early days of the convict transports by the unfortunate Captain Cairnes. Having deposited the Merinos safely in the colony, Captain Cairnes was homeward bound when his ship was captured by pirates in the Atlantic Ocean. Tragically, his children were also on board and the entire family were made to walk the plank and drowned.

No record exists of William Campbell's occupation at Ghinghinda, but it is unlikely that he was an itinerant shearer or station hand, as these men would generally have been accommodated in the barrack-like conditions of the shearers' or hands' huts, which were very basic dormitories and certainly no place for women. The job of the station hand was to assist in mustering the sheep for shearing, and with general labouring duties. Generally, only the more senior or skilled employees would have been afforded the opportunity of bringing their wives and children with them. In all likelihood William Campbell was employed as an overseer or boundary rider, engaged by the station owner to ride around the boundary of the station on horseback, looking after and maintaining the fences and generally keeping an eye on the furthest reaches of his Master's property. Sarah would have been expected to work too, perhaps as a cook or laundress, or as a domestic servant in the manager's house, though she would have had to keep James with her at all times, as there would not have been anyone else to care for him.

Ghinghinda was bleak, isolated and remote. The neighbouring stations of Broadmere, Bungeban, Coorada, Glenhaughton, Gwambagwine, Hornet Bank, Kinnoul, Lilyvale or Palm Tree were all hours away on horseback. Over five hundred kilometres away from bustling industrialised Brisbane, it might as well have been five thousand. In his famous book, *On the Wool Track*, written in 1910, CEW Bean described the landscape thus: *"However far you search for the Outback, there seems to be always an Outback beyond."*[45] You could travel for hundreds of miles without coming across as much as a fence, let alone an abandoned homestead or shepherd's hut. Human habitation of vast swathes of the back country was only possible because of a network of water tanks constructed by the early settlers to water their sheep and cattle. At the same time,

45   *On the Wool Track*, CEW Bean, London, 1910 p. ix.

however, overgrazing of the land caused untold damage, leading to soil erosion, which in turn contributed to flooding when the rains did eventually arrive.

Travelling across this landscape was fraught with danger for the unprepared or the simply unlucky. Although a man could reasonably expect to travel from water tank to water tank until he reached a settlement or station, as Bean pointed out, if some accident befell him and he suffered injury or lost his water bottle, *"He has as much chance as a polar explorer would have if the same thing happened to him near the South Pole."*[46] The discovery of some poor long-dead soul by the wayside was, unfortunately, a regular occurrence.

For children living in the outback, the hazards were magnified a thousand times over. So many simply succumbed to heat stroke and the burning sun, or became ill with waterborne diseases such as cholera and dysentery, particularly during prolonged spells of very wet weather. Some were bitten by snakes or spiders, others could be attacked or taken by dingoes. A few were trampled by horses or cattle, fell down gullies or off cliffs. It was not unheard of for small children to wander away from their homes, never to be seen again. Bean recalls one 1880s account of two small children from Bourke in New South Wales who wandered off on the way home from school. With the aid of aboriginal trackers, the children were found alive but in a very poor condition a few days later, some thirty eight miles away.[47] Queensland is a beautiful but harsh country, treating with contempt the ignorant, the unprepared, the foolhardy and most of all, the careless.

Every parent is familiar with that sensation of blind panic, that heart-stopping moment when a small child lets go of their hand and in the blink of an eye and a tangle of legs is gone, perhaps in a crowded park beside the swings or in the queue for ice-creams, perhaps in a busy supermarket or in the throngs

---

46 Ibid p. 7.
47 Ibid pp. 6–7.

of people "oohing and ahhing" at fireworks display or the illuminations in the high street at Christmas.

For a few seconds or minutes all logic and reason disappear and they search frantically, pushing their way past human obstacles, all sorts of ridiculous thoughts about the possible ills that could have befallen their child galloping through their minds, constantly repeating the same question to indifferent strangers, "Have you seen my boy?" Inevitably, the small person reappears, having been momentarily distracted by a beach ball, a friendly dog, or a brightly lit glittering display in a shop window, and immediately the parent is overwhelmed with relief. Equally inevitably, the small person is scolded for wandering off, and his mother or father holds his tiny hot hand a little more tightly.

"Have you seen my boy?"

On the morning of 23rd May 1891, little James Campbell could not be found. There was no one else around for Sarah to ask. Perhaps James had wandered off back towards the cottage, having caught sight of his father rounding up the livestock in the stock pens in the distance. Perhaps he'd got his eye on a small bird pecking at the grubs and insects in the bushes and had decided to investigate further, or had found a muddy puddle in which to jump and splash or poke about in with a small stick. Maybe this tiny boy had decided to play a game of hide and seek with his mother, and had concealed himself under the washing basket or wrapped himself in the freshly-laundered wet sheets, giggling to himself as his mother called for him, ready to shout "boo!" when he was finally discovered. As every parent knows, small children possess a very unnerving talent for hiding.

"Have you seen my boy?"

Sarah called for James over and over. She could not hear any shouts of "Mama!". She could not be hearing him laughing or chattering away to himself as mischievous two year olds are wont to do. There was no sound of him whimpering or crying, as would be expected if he'd fallen and scraped his knee or caught his shirt on a thorny twig and become stuck fast in the bushes, or stumbled upon the prickly burrs that covered the earth down towards the creek. Sarah's calls were met with silence.

Amongst Aunt Edie's box of photographs and letters, there is not one photograph of Sarah, nor a single letter written in her hand to her family back home in County Durham. There are no photographs of baby James. There is nothing which might indicate how Sarah looked or spoke or felt, what she believed in or what motivated her, what was important to her or what her opinions might be. Despite this she seems familiar to me, like an old friend. I know Sarah. In the course of my research into her story, I stumbled upon the only record still in existence of her words and thoughts, and the only surviving evidence of her signature. It doesn't amount to very much. It's a simple handwritten document consisting of only two pages, which describes the events of the morning of 23rd May 1891.

"Have you seen my boy?"

The document isn't a journal or diary entry, or a long-forgotten letter, which has been languishing in another attaché case on the other side of the world, as one might expect. These two short manuscript pages contain the witness statement which Sarah gave to Mr Robert Alexander, having travelled down from the station at Ghinghinda to the county town of Taroom two days later. Mr Alexander was the local police magistrate and Justice of the Peace.

These are Sarah's words.

"On Saturday this 23rd instant, I was washing at Ghinghinda Creek.
The child was with me.
I left him standing on the bank of the creek and went to the line with some clothes.
When I looked round from the line I could not see him.
I called him by his name, and got no reply.
I then ran down to the bank and found him in the water.
He was on the top of the water, but was not moving.

His clothes kept him up.
I took him out and found he was dead.
I carried him up to his father at the station where he was working.
The child was a little over 2 years old."

Signed – Sarah Campbell

The death certificate attached to the statement records the cause of death as "drowning, accidental".

The panic and terror that must have overcome Sarah as she spotted the little body in the water are almost unimaginable. The statement she gave to the coroner is, as is the very nature of legal documents, brief and to the point, matter of fact, cold and unemotional, with no hint of the grief and shock and sheer anguish she was unquestionably suffering.

I read the statement over and over again, turning the events over in my mind. One sentence in particular haunted me. "*I carried him up to his father at the station where he was working.*"

I imagined William, busy in the stockyards, laughing and joking with the farmhands, giving out orders, perhaps swearing under his breath at a particularly stubborn ewe or repairing the fences, looking up from his work and smiling as he saw his young wife approaching in the middle distance, their son in her arms. I imagined the colour draining from his face as Sarah drew closer and he could see her sobbing hysterically, the soaking wet bundle in her arms, motionless. I imagined William running towards her, taking the child from her, shaking him, and making fruitless efforts to revive him. And worst of all, I imagined William screaming at his wife on account of her negligence, berating her for not looking after the boy properly, and for allowing him to play alone on the bank of the creek, turning her back upon him while she went to peg out the washing.

James Campbell was dead. The awful, inescapable truth was

that Sarah, by virtue of her inattention and carelessness, was to blame.

Taroom is a small town, about fifty miles south of Ghinghinda, deep in the heart of the Queensland back country. I wondered about Sarah's journey there to report her boy's death to the authorities, accompanied by William – perhaps one of the farm hands or another of the station owner Mr Mayne's staff drove them there in the wagon; maybe William drove them there himself in their horse and cart, the little body in a home-made coffin on the back, the stony silence punctuated only with the noise of the horses' hooves on the rocky track, with birdsong, and with occasional sobbing. The arrival of the Campbells in Taroom was recorded in the local newspaper:

> *"On the morning of the 26th a baggy came into town from Ghinghinda, containing the remains of an infant 18 months old, the son of people of the name of Campbell. In the absence of the mother the little one had strayed away and fallen into a waterhole, and life was extinct before they found him."*[48]

How the dread in Sarah's heart must have increased with each passing mile. Did she worry that she might be held to blame for the child's death? Would her account be believed by the magistrate? Might he suggest that it was not in fact an accident and that she had intended to harm the child? Shame. Fear. Anxiety. Guilt.

Reading Sarah's words for the first time was spine tingling, not least because of the terrible circumstances in which they were recorded. I read her statement over and over again, and imagined her still in shock, sat in front of the magistrate Mr Alexander, attempting to recount the events of that May morning. I read the words aloud, and could hear Sarah's County Durham accent echoed in my own. I could hear her voice

---

48   *The Week*, Brisbane, Queensland, 12th June 1891 www.trove.nla.gov.au

wavering as the words stuck in her throat while she choked back the tears. I could see William, standing behind her, stern-faced and grief-stricken, one hand placed on his wife's shoulder, the other clutching his dirt-stained and dusty hat, and I wondered if he ever found it within himself to forgive her.

We can only guess at the impact of James' death on Sarah and William's relationship. Did William bring it up again every time they had a disagreement? Or was he warm and supportive and did they share the burden of their grief? Of course, infant mortality was a fact of life in those days, and deaths by drowning (particularly of children) were very common, especially in those areas where the creeks and rivers were swollen by flooding. In 1896, just five years after James' death, the major causes of death in Queensland were tuberculosis and pneumonia, but drowning accounted for one hundred and fifty-nine deaths in that year alone. Thirty-one per cent of all male deaths in that year were in the under fives, and twenty-six per cent of all deaths were in the first year of life.[49] However, to consider any one family's loss in terms of simple statistics is to negate the pain and anguish they undoubtedly felt.

How many times did Sarah relive that moment, in her nightmares and in her daydreams? Upon waking each morning, she must have experienced that wave of grief, that knot of angst and guilt in her chest for the rest of her days. How do you live with that? How do you continue to go about your daily life knowing that one brief moment of carelessness, a few seconds of inattention, a momentary distraction has led to the death of your child?

After burying James in the little cemetery at Taroom, Sarah could not face returning to Ghinghinda. The Campbells left that desolate spot behind at the first opportunity, and headed south-east to the huge sheep station at Jondaryan to look for work.

Although she did not know it, at the time of James' death, Sarah was pregnant.

---

49 *Queensland Past and Present:100 Years of Statistics 1886-1996*, Ch.8 Health, Section 5 pp. 263–270.

12

Jondaryan

Sarah Campbell gave birth to her second son, named William John (Bill), after his father, on 28th February 1892, almost nine months to the day after little James' death, at East Prairie on the Darling Downs. At that time, East Prairie was part of the massive Jondaryan sheep station, and the location of two boundary riders' cottages.[50] Whether as the result of a difficult pregnancy that left Sarah unable or unwilling to bear any further children, or as a consequence of the traumatic circumstances of James' death which may have caused a rift in their marriage, there were no more babies for William and Sarah. Unusually for the time, Bill Campbell was to grow up as an only child.

Life on the Jondaryan Station could not have been more different to the isolated and lonely existence Sarah had led deep in the outback at Ghinghinda. For a start, since the 1860s, Jondaryan had been connected to Brisbane by rail (via the nearest town of any significant size, Toowoomba) when the railways were extended out to the Darling Downs and beyond. Throughout the latter half of the nineteenth century, the tendrils of the railways spread ever westwards. Human cargo, however, was not the priority – there was only one reason for the expansion of the railways, and that was to ensure that the prized Australian merino wool was got as quickly to the ports for export around the Empire (but also to France and Germany) as was humanly

---

50 I am grateful to Wendy King and the staff at Jondaryan for this information.

possible. Prior to this, every conceivable method of transport was utilised to ensure the newly-sheared wool reached its destination quickly and in time for the wool sales in the cities – river boats, wagons and horses, bullock carts and even camels were employed.

Jondaryan was situated in the heart of the Darling Downs, and was prime grazing country, though very prone to the vagaries of the climate. As in much of Queensland, severe floods were frequently preceded by years of drought. Prior to settlement, the Downs had been covered in wild oats and grasses five to six feet tall, which rendered vast swathes of land almost impenetrable.

When the interior of Australia began to be opened up for settlement in the 1840s and 1850s, huge areas were grabbed by the so-called "squatters" – generally young men from rich or upper-class British families who saw an incredible opportunity to accumulate even more wealth from grazing sheep and cattle and from the burgeoning wool industry. In return, they paid the New South Wales (as it was then) government a nominal fee per acre. Having made their fortune, many returned "home" to Britain, but a few stayed and became, in effect, the Australian gentry. Eventually much of the land was repurchased by the Queensland and other state governments in the latter half of the nineteenth century, and divided up into small farms or "selections" and sold to famers and homesteaders, known as "selectors". Hence the title of Steele Rudd's book, *On Our Selection.*

Jondaryan station is described in the 1920 book *Fox's History of Queensland* thus:

> "A large station which originally contained 155,000 acres, mostly splendidly-grassed open downs, carrying 140,000 sheep and 2000 head of cattle."

By the time that book had been written, the station had been broken up and large parts of it sold off to small farmers and dairymen, however when the Campbells moved there in 1891/1892, Jondaryan was at its peak.

Like many of the larger stations, Jondaryan was owned by wealthy British investors, William Kent (and after his death by his trustees) and Edward Wienholt. Kent and Wienholt had paid Robert Tooth the huge sum of £108,000 for the property in 1863, the equivalent of around £9,500,000 today.[51] Often these wealthy gentlemen didn't live on their stations, and were absentee landlords, preferring to live nearer to "civilisation" in the cities, or in Wienholt's case, back in England, in the Lake District. Some barely even visited their properties, leaving them in the hands of trusted managers. Those who did choose to reside on their stations lived the life of an English country squire, often in very grand, lavishly-furnished homes, a far cry from the barrack-like bunk rooms of the shearers or the slab huts of their married employees. Fletcher, in his *Colonial Australia Before 1850*, written in 1876,[52] describes how these station owners lived like English gentry, filled their houses with costly imported furniture, employed servants and governesses for their children, kept stables of thoroughbred horses, and entertained those of their class lavishly.

A wonderfully detailed account of life on the station, as Sarah Campbell would have encountered it, appears in Jan Walker's superb social history, *Jondaryan Station: The Relationship between Pastoral Capital and Pastoral Labour.*[53] Walker compares life on the larger stations to the close-knit hierarchical structure of a rural English village. Certainly, some station owners took their part as the "Lord of the Manor" very seriously, with the result that many of the lowest order of their employees were treated little better than serfs or bonded labour. This was particularly true of the shepherds and labourers, who were often Aborigines

51 "Jondaryan, Last of Big Downs Stations", *Queensland Country Life*, 10th January 1946, www.nla.gov.au/nla.newsarticle97144826.
52 *Colonial Australia before 1850*, B. Fletcher, Melbourne, Nelson, 1876.
53 Jondaryan Station: The Relationship between Pastoral Capital and Pastoral Labour, Jan Walker, (University of Queensland Press), 1988.

or Chinese, Melanesian and Indian immigrants; these poor souls had little or no social status, and were very much seen as being at the bottom of the heap, with no prospect of promotion or any increase in their meagre wages. Walker describes how, by 1877, Edward Wienholt and the Trustees of William Kent were the largest owners of freehold land in Queensland, and Jondaryan was the largest freehold run. I prefer to think of the station owners as Australian equivalents of the Londonderrys, the owners of Seaham and the Rainton pits – both had incredible wealth, built on the backs of the poor, the working classes, and the lowest strata of society; both completely controlled and exploited the lives of their employees and their families, treating them as commodities, the means to an end.

Given its size, Jondaryan soon developed into a large village, with one of the largest and most advanced woodsheds in Queensland; with rows of cottages for those employees who were married or who had dependents, a blacksmith's shop, a wheelwright, a store, bunk houses for the men, an overseer's cottage, which would have been set slightly apart from the other cottages, to reflect the social status of the occupant; a schoolhouse, a large and spacious home for the manager and of course the owner's mansion, the Jondaryan homestead. This luxurious dwelling had a large garden, a swimming hole, and even its own vineyard.

When Sarah and William Campbell moved to Jondaryan, the station was managed by the formidable William Graham, who ran the property on behalf of the owners for over forty years until his death in 1913. In that time, the population on the station had risen to around two hundred, although during shearing season this could increase to three hundred and fifty, perhaps even four hundred, with the influx of shearers and seasonal workers. Lambing traditionally took place between August and September, washing in mid-September, with shearing in early October until the middle of December, but by the time the Campbells had moved there, such was the number of sheep that the station was actually shearing twice a year, in September and October, and then in March and April. The fact that Bill Campbell was born on the station in February 1892 lends further weight to the argument that his father William was not a shearer – had he been so it is unlikely that Sarah would have accompanied him, nor that he would have been on the station between shearing seasons.

As the station population expanded, so did the requirement for domestic labour, and more women were recruited to work on the station as domestic servants, seamstresses, nurses, laundry women, kitchen maids and cooks. On Bill Campbell's birth certificate, Sarah's profession is once again given as "domestic servant" – like the other station wives, it's very likely that she would have ended up cooking, working as a washer woman or cleaning and looking after the shearers' and single men's bunk houses. Despite all her adventures, it seems that Sarah had never been able to escape her life of drudgery. According to Jan Walker, up to around 1875 any women who worked on Jondaryan were usually employed as cooks; thereafter, up until around 1893 when the station began slowly to decline, they worked as servants, and could have expected to earn perhaps £20 per year if they were lucky. However, it would be wrong to think that there was anything even approaching equality of numbers between the sexes on the station – the average number of women employed between 1866 and 1893 was only ten, and they were outnumbered by the men thirty to one. It was thought that the presence of women on the station had a "civilising" effect on the menfolk, helping to eradicate the "evils of prostitution and homosexuality".[54] The wives of the managers and most senior employees enjoyed a very different lifestyle to the rest of the station women, with constant rounds of visiting each other's grand houses, parties and entertaining, living the lives of fine English ladies, which is precisely how they behaved and were treated.

---

54   Ibid pp. 85–88.

The station owners, through their managers – men like William Graham – exerted a huge level of influence and control over the everyday lives of their employees. Workers could be fined up to five shillings per day for being off sick or for being late, for example if a child was ill; shepherds were frequently fined for the loss of or injury to sheep. Shearers could lose wages for bad shearing if a sheep was cut; sometimes overseers would refuse to pay the shearers that day's wages altogether, which was a crafty method of having work done for nothing and lowering the wage bill.

Life on Jondaryan wasn't all work and no play however. Entertainments for the workers were often provided, such as concerts, educational lectures, and travelling shows and even circuses would occasionally stop by. A cricket club had been formed in 1877, and there was a church which ran a Sunday school for the children. Jondaryan, like every station, held a shearers' feast to celebrate the end of the shearing season. All employees and contractors were invited, together with the families of the married men, the managers and guests of rank from neighbouring stations. There would be horse races, a picnic, and dancing in the evening in the woolshed, not dissimilar to kind of parties and picnics the Londonderrys hosted at Seaham Hall for the miners and their families. Jondaryan may have been over ten thousand miles from Seaham but the same social class distinctions and structures prevailed.

Despite this, all was not well on the station. Sarah and William's arrival at Jondarayan coincided with the aftermath of the most turbulent period in the station's short history, and an infamous episode which would ultimately result in the station's decline in the mid-1890s. Not for the first time, Sarah found herself caught up in bitter industrial unrest.

Increasing discontent with wages and conditions throughout Queensland and New South Wales during the 1880s had led to the formation of various workers' associations and the growth of the trade union movement. Conditions at Jondaryan in particular were criticised.

"If anything can show the need of a shearers' association, it is the treatment of men at this station.... They are not regarded as men at all but as machines."[55]

In May 1890, the shearers of Jondarayan had had enough, and went out on strike. This was not particularly unusual in itself – strikes were nothing new in the era of organised labour – but what was different about the Jondaryan Incident, as it became known, was that the impact was felt far and wide throughout Queensland. The 1890 sheep shearers' strike was a battle of wills between the unions and the station owners. Emboldened by the growth in strength and numbers, and possibly wanting to pick a fight, the Shearers' Association insisted that the owners should employ only unionised labour at Jondaryan; naturally the owners resisted, arguing that they had the right to employ whomsoever they wished. Much like the managers of Seaham Colliery had done ten years before during the strike which followed the 1880 explosion, the owners tried to bring in blackleg labour to ensure that production levels were maintained. The parties' respective positions appeared entrenched but the shearers soon gained the upper hand when the strike spread. Carriers refused to take non-union wool to the railway stations for transport to the ports; what little wool did reach the dockside warehouses stayed there, as the dockers refused to load wool which had been produced by non-union labour. The station owners found themselves between a rock and a hard place, and had no option but to meet the demands of the Shearers' Association.

Although the shearers had won a famous victory in 1890, their success was not to be repeated when they attempted to pull off the same feat the following year. By this time the station owners had become much more organised and had set up their own trade organisations to counter the power of the trade unions. The worsening economic conditions, combined with several successive years of severe flooding which had a

55 *Toowoomba Chronicle*, 14th November 1875, cited by Jan Walker, ibid.

devastating effect on many stations, meant that increasing numbers of shearers were unwilling to risk their jobs by becoming involved in industrial action. The power of the shearers' unions began to diminish as their membership fell, but the workers of Queensland began to take on the fight in a different arena. New legislation allowed for the payment of a salary to members of parliament, which in turn paved the way for "working men" to give up their jobs and stand for election. The first Labour MP was elected to the Queensland parliament in 1893, and the fortunes of the labour movement and the party it spawned would wax and wane for decades.

The Jondaryan Incident had perhaps tarnished the reputation of that station forever. By the mid-1890s, the population of the station had declined to fifty-five permanent employees, with perhaps as few as thirty or forty itinerant workers and shearers arriving for the shearing season. Over the coming years, various parts of the station were sold off to farmers and selectors. What is left endures as a tourist attraction these days – you can still visit Jondaryan, learn about its history and even get married in the wool shed which William Campbell knew so well.

But what became of William and Sarah and little Bill?

13

At the Foot of the Mountain

Infuriatingly, the Campbells disappeared from public and documentary record for the next eight years. From the date of Bill's birth in February 1892 at East Prairie, I could find no trace of William or Sarah. There were no further births recorded, nor were there any deaths. I could not determine whether they remained at Jondaryan or whether they moved on to a different station, or perhaps even returned to Brisbane. There are no entries in trade directories, nor was there any mention of William in the electoral registers, which were compiled roughly every ten years or so, which suggests that he was not a property owner and therefore not qualified to vote when the 1893 register was compiled. The trail had gone cold.

However, from re-reading Bill's letters to his Seaham cousin Edie, I knew that the family must have settled at Tamborine Mountain in the late 1890s or early 1900s. There is no explanation in the letters as to why the family chose that particular spot, or what drew them there. Perhaps William had been working nearby; perhaps they already had friends and connections there. Maybe the land, covered in rainforest, was yet to be cleared and therefore cheap.

Within distant sight of the city lights and the high rises of the Gold Coast and Surfer's Paradise, Mt. Tamborine is a popular tourist destination, part of the chain of mountains and ranges that make up the so-called "Scenic Rim" area. Its beauty and climate (Tamborine is around five degrees cooler than the coastal plains) were attracting visitors even at the turn of the twentieth century, and the area became a favourite of weekend trippers from Brisbane, and of VIPs, artists and writers, who came to experience the rainforest and the stunning coastal vistas. Though the Mountain was still very sparsely populated, boarding houses began to spring up to service the visitors, as at that time it was impossible to travel to Brisbane and back in a day. One of the most notable of these boarding houses was Capo di Monte, an elegant two-storied villa in the colonial style; another was St Bernard's, which enjoys an enviable position on a mountain shelf at the head of the Guanaba Gorge, looking down towards the Pacific, surrounded by palm trees and echoing to the screeches of the cockatoos overhead. The St Bernard's Hotel still looks after guests today.

The mountain is still surrounded by rolling hills and downland, fertile farmland, nature reserves and national parks. The plateau is peppered with discreetly expensive homes, trendy cafes and upmarket restaurants, art galleries, vineyards and boutique accommodation for the discerning visitor. There are rainforest walks and picturesque picnic spots, glittering glow-worm caves and sparkling waterfalls, botanic gardens and exclusive day spas, cheesemakers and fudge makers, microbreweries and even a distillery.

In the course of my correspondence with Campbells' descendants in Queensland, I was contacted by Iain Hollindale, who very kindly sent me a copy of his wonderful book, *Life and Cricket on the Coomera*,[56] which sets out the history of the game in the region from the time of the earliest settlers in the late nineteenth century. The book contains some wonderful photographs of life in and around Tamborine and Coomera in the early twentieth century. Intriguingly, at the front of the book, there is a map from 1900 showing the position of the seven

---

56   *Life and Cricket on the Coomera: A Journey Through 140 years of Cricket, Life and History along Queensland's Coomera River*, Ian Hollindale, Australia, 2008.

cricket pitches used by the Coomera Cricket Club (now firmly settled at Hope Island) over the decades. The map also shows in detail the names of all the landowners in the area, with each individual plot clearly marked. In the bottom left hand corner, almost at the edge of the page, in the district of Guanaba, at the very foot of the eastern slopes of Tamborine Mountain, is an almost rectangular plot, criss-crossed with creeks. Bordered to the north by land owned by the Binsteads, to the west by the Wilsons, and to the south by the Stuarts, it is clearly marked "W J Campbell". The Hollindale family still own land adjoining what was the Campbell farm; one of the elderly aunts, now in her nineties, can still recall the Campbells.

I spent hours poring over current day maps and plans and satellite images, and was eventually able to locate the site of William and Sarah's farm, not too far from where the perfectly-manicured greens and fairways of Mt. Tamborine Golf Club lie now, and accessed via a steep and winding narrow road from the St Bernard's area of the mountain, at the bottom of a narrow-wooded lane now known as Sherlock Court. The plot of land where the farm was situated has barely changed in a hundred years – perhaps there are a few more houses in the surrounding area (the eighty acres of the Campbell farm having been divided up into smaller plots), tarmacked roads, the golf club, the odd pylon and telegraph post, and in the distance the thriving little village which snakes along the mountain top. The silhouette of the mountain itself, its slopes cloaked in dense rainforest to the north, and eucalyptus forest to the east, would still be recognisable to William and Sarah and Bill today.

In Edie's box of photographs, there is a picture of Bill Campbell taken in the early 1920s. In the photograph Bill, in white cotton trousers, shirtsleeves rolled up, is lifting a crop of potatoes with the help of one of his horses. In the background, beyond a rough wooden shack with a two-tone corrugated roof and the forest, the unmistakeable shape of Tamborine Mountain sweeps gently downwards.

Mount Tamborine is still an idyllic spot, a leafy paradise teeming with life. When the Campbells arrived there at the end of the nineteenth century, the western slopes of the mountain were still cloaked in shimmering forests of eucalyptus; on the eastern slopes, gum trees – silver gums, bloodwoods and grey barks – jostled for position with cedars and beech. Lazy carpet pythons made their homes in the hollows of rotting logs, whilst the forest echoed to the sound of birdsong. Wild turkeys, cink lizards and wallabies scuttled around in the undergrowth; further east in the Guanaba area, koalas munched quietly in the canopy above them.

Despite its close proximity to Brisbane – just under fifty miles or so – Mount Tamborine was not settled until around 1875. Timber cutting had begun in 1862, but without any great success. The lack of any access roads meant that many of the logs lay rotting where they had been felled, until a means was devised to send the logs down the mountain using the streams and waterfalls. A water-powered sawmill was eventually constructed by the Curtis family. Curtis Falls were named for them and are a popular tourist attraction today. Their descendants still live on the mountain.

Although much of the land on and around the mountain was selected (divided up into plots to be leased from the Queensland government, and after a fixed period of occupation and evidence that the land had been "improved", ownership was transferred to the selector) early attempts to establish a community floundered, not least due to the difficulty of access, there being no roads, the density of the rainforest and the maze of creeks and gullies. In the late nineteenth century, Tamborine was still a very isolated spot. As a result, land there was cheaper than near the already established settlements or where clearing of the rainforest for agriculture and grazing had already taken place. Maybe that's why the Campbells chose to settle there. It's also possible that they ended up at Tamborine as there was simply no other land left in the area – all the decent flat open farmland surrounding the mountain had already been taken up by selectors decades before William and Sarah reached the area.

Beautiful as it was, Tamborine was no Garden of Eden, and far from the earthly paradise it is today. Life on and around the mountain for the Campbells and the other early settlers was brutal. Many of the early selectors gave up at the first attempt, the density of the forest proving too great an obstacle to their ambitions; others managed to establish small farms only to see their crops and orchards wither and fail, after year upon year of drought or flood; others still could grow barely enough to feed their families. Only very small areas could be cleared at a time – although the soil was fertile enough, these shady rainforest clearings were difficult to farm as the sunlight barely penetrated the dense tree canopy which towered above them.[57]

Clearing the land to create farmland or pasture was probably the most difficult, the most back-breaking and the first task the selectors encountered. The ancient rainforest had to be felled, by hand, using saws and axes, tree by tree, the undergrowth hacked away to expose the bare earth, and the remaining stumps burned away. Smoke from the burning-off would have been visible for miles around – care had to be taken not to cause bush fires in hot weather and times of drought. It could take days, even weeks, to clear a patch of just a few square yards. Once the soil had been exposed, any large rocks and stones had to be painstakingly removed, and the earth broken up with picks or ploughs, if selectors had access to one.

Whilst the land was being cleared, the family would have had no income. Perhaps William laboured for neighbours on adjoining farms in return for help with the logging, clearing and burning. Some would-be farmers would spend a few weeks clearing their land then return to work in the city for a while, or go off shearing for a few months to earn extra money. Like the other families who arrived to farm on the mountain, Sarah,

---

57   *A Land of Hills and Valleys – Tamborine Mountain 1875-1914*, Eve Curtis, published in Queensland Heritage.

William and their child slept out under canvas for weeks on end, their couple of horses tethered nearby. They endured extremes of weather from torrential, unremitting downpours and violent thunderstorms, when it was impossible to keep themselves and their belongings dry, to searing heat with temperatures occasionally hitting the high thirties, until enough trees had been felled and a suitable spot chosen upon which to construct a slab hut from cut timber.

Much of the land on the edge of the Campbell plot was too steep to be cleared, or to be of any use for farming, and remains covered in forest to this day. In the damp weather the mosquitoes were unrelenting, and there was an ever-present threat from venomous snakes and spiders. Heat stroke was very common and not infrequently fatal. As well as the physical hardships, Sarah would have had to cope with a crushing sense of loneliness. In the early days, she hardly saw another soul, apart from William and Bill, for days, sometimes weeks at a time. Female company was very hard to come by.

For the family home, William chose a raised, level spot, where the steep mountainside gives way to gentle hills and then begins to flatten out towards the Coomera River, overlooking the creek. After months of "camping out" the family moved into the two-roomed slab cottage, with its wooden planked walls, wooden shutters for windows, and shingle roof which overhung the little building, providing a shaded porch area outside, which ran the length of the cottage.

At one end, there was a chimney recess and a basic fireplace constructed from stones formed into a square, upon which Sarah would have prepared all of the family meals. Over the years, the cottage would eventually be extended to accommodate Bill's family. There was no plumbing, no water, no drainage and no heating, the only light coming from candles or oil lamps. A crude earth closet in a small wooden shed round the back of the property provided the only toilet facilities. The cottage was dark but cool, and with the addition of a kitchen table, several chairs, a bedstead, shelves, a handful of photographs of family back in England, and a few knick-knacks, soon began to feel homelier. Nonetheless, it was a far cry from the solid County Durham terraced miners' cottages where Sarah had been brought up.

Once a sufficiently large area of land had been cleared, the task of planting began. Grass seed had to be sown to create pasture for grazing for cows and sheep; other areas were ploughed by horses and planted with crops such as wheat, potatoes, pumpkins and other vegetables. On sunny slopes, rows of fruit trees were dug in to create orchards of apples, oranges, lemons and plums. Of course, it would be several years before the orchards were mature and producing fruit in sufficient quantities to take to market. Some farmers experimented with sugar cane and arrowroot, and for a few decades there was a thriving sugar cane industry along the Coomera River. Other farmers on Tamborine switched to flower cultivation, and for years supplied Brisbane with fresh cut flowers transported in wooden boxes.

The construction of an assortment of sheds and stables soon followed, with a small "dairy" for the milking of the cows William had purchased from a farmer in Upper Coomera. A team of horses was brought in to assist with the ploughing and timber hauling, as well as being the family's only means of transport.

A million miles from the coal dust and the bitter industrial disputes of Seaham and Rainton and Page Bank; a million miles from the hustle and bustle of Brisbane; a million miles from Ghinghinda and the graveyard at Taroom where the tiny body of James Campbell was laid to rest; a million miles from the sheep shearers and their strikes at Jondaryan – Sarah Campbell had finally found "home".

The more I learned about Sarah's life on the farm, the more one particular question began to plague me. After all the tragedy and hardship she had experienced in her life, was she finally happy there? The life of a farmer's wife was incredibly hard. As well as helping out with the farm work, the milking, skimming off the cream, making butter by hand in a butter churn, and feeding the animals, Sarah would have had to attend to all the usual household duties – cooking, baking, cleaning, laundry and looking after Bill, reading to him and perhaps teaching him his alphabet and counting, at least until he was old enough to travel to school in Maudsland with the other farmers' children. Sarah's years at the Village Farmhouse in Seaton would have stood her in good stead – at least she knew how to milk cows and look after a dairy herd.

In reality, Sarah's life was little changed from when she was a maid-of-all-work, although there was one significant difference. Now she was answerable to no one but her husband. For the first time in her life, she was her own mistress, jointly responsible for eighty acres of pasture and woodland, a herd of dairy cows, a handful of horses and pigs, numerous hens, several wagons and carts, as well as crops of potatoes, wheat and vegetables, an orchard of fruit trees, and not to mention a small boy. The electoral roll of 1903 records that both Sarah and William were now landowners and therefore eligible to vote – an opportunity which would not be available to Sarah's sisters back in England for another fifteen years.

Was she happy with her lot? Did she reflect daily that her decision to leave England behind had been the right one? Or did she stand at the door of her cottage every morning, gazing out at the little creek in front of the house, listening to the screech of parrots and cockatoos, and the song of lyrebirds and lorakeets, yearning for County Durham and the stiff North Sea breeze that rustles through the tree tops in Seaton? Did she long for the company of the friends and neighbours she had left behind in the village, the Bolands, Hodgsons, Armbristers and Thompsons? Did she miss chatting to the girls who worked behind the bar in the Dun Cow, and the farm labourers and miners who frequented that establishment? Perhaps she recalled with fondness her weekly trips into Seaham Colliery or down to the shops in Church Street and Adelaide Row in Seaham Harbour, gossiping with the other servant girls on errands for their mistresses as she stocked up on provisions and ran messages for Mrs Boland. Did Sarah still experience the pangs of homesickness and an ache for the sisters and mother she knew she would never see again? Perhaps she was content and had no regrets, confident that despite all she had endured, her life choices had been the correct ones.

Undeterred by the hardships, the floods, the droughts, and the cycle of boom and bust which plagued Queensland in the 1890s and early 1900s, Sarah and William Campbell accomplished what so many others had failed to achieve, and made a success of the farm.

The Campbells were never wealthy – perhaps never even comfortably off – but they never went hungry and were able to make a decent enough living from selling their farm produce on the mountain and in Upper Coomera. William also ran a haulage business with his horse and cart, carrying goods, fruit and vegetables from friends and neighbours to be sold up in North Tamborine village on the mountain, and down to Siganto's wharf at Upper Coomera, bringing in much-needed supplies which arrived from Brisbane and further afield on the return journey. The milk and cream from the Campbells' cows was sold daily to the big Brisbane dairies. Amongst Edie's photographs there is a picture of the old-fashioned metal cream churns being sent across the Coomera River by means of a rope and pulley system when the river was in flood, which seems to have been a regular occurrence. The tiny cemetery at Upper Coomera is filled with the bones of those who drowned in the numerous perilous floods that plagued this riverside community.

The Coomera River was the lifeblood of this small corner of Queensland, with goods, people, mail and livestock ferried into Siganto's wharf from Brisbane and the Queensland ports on a daily basis. Indeed, it is likely that William and Sarah initially arrived in the area by steamboat, with all of their possessions bundled up into trunks and tea chests, perhaps staying in Upper Coomera for a few days to purchase transport and provisions before making the short journey along the river banks to Guanaba and the lower reaches of Tamborine to inspect their land for the first time.

The work of a farmer's wife was never done, but still Sarah somehow found time to keep up with her correspondence. She continued to write regularly to her mother, sisters, cousins, nephews and nieces in England, handing her letters to William for him to drop off at the little post office in Upper Coomera when he was making his deliveries in the cart, or sending them up the mountain to Mrs Geissman who ran a post office from the St Bernard's Hotel.

Towards the end of May 1900 Sarah received a letter from her brother-in-law James Hudson, informing her of the death of her younger sister Ann at the age of thirty-four, just a few weeks before. Ann left behind James and six children, the youngest of whom was barely a year old. Sarah's widowed mother Margaret and her youngest sister Fanny had of course gone to live with Ann and James not long after their marriage in 1886, in their cottage at Grindon Mill in Sunderland. By the time of Ann's death, Fanny had gone into service; the Hudson children were brought up by their Granny Margaret. The Hudson family were hit by a further tragedy just five years later, when Ann and James' son, Thomas, (named after his grandfather, the horsekeeper Thomas Marshall) died at the age of fourteen. Sarah was not alone in her grief for her lost son James; several of the Marshall sisters knew the pain of the loss of a child. Margaret lost a daughter, Isabella, aged five in 1903; Fanny's first daughter died shortly after birth, a year or so before Edie was born in 1906.

It is unlikely that Sarah left the farm and ventured up to the small but growing settlement on the mountain top very often. A visit to the top of Tamborine necessitated a trek up a treacherous and incredibly steep mountain track, first through eucalyptus forest and scrub and then through the rainforest. It is more probable that on the rare occasion she went out and about, she visited neighbours and acquaintances elsewhere in the Guanaba district and Upper Coomera (the Campbells always gave their address as Guanaba or Coomera, rather than Tamborine). Perhaps occasional trips were made to the small seaside town at Southport around seventeen miles distant, which had a wider range of facilities than Upper Coomera, including a doctor, a library, a small selection of shops, hotels, guesthouses and a delightful beach, and in later years a theatre, a pier and amusements. Southport today is the central business district of the City of Gold Coast, which simply did not exist until the late 1950s. In 1900, it was already a fashionable seaside resort, where steamers from Brisbane would discharge visitors keen to enjoy the sea air, the swimming pools and a spot of fishing.

Bill Campbell had an idyllic childhood growing up on the farm. There he learned, when a very small boy, how to feed the hens and gather eggs, which snakes were harmless and which would bite, how to gather fruit from the orchard, how to milk a cow and churn butter, and later how to ride, how to look after the horses and livestock, how to groom the horses and clean the tack, how to plough and plant seeds and harvest the crops, the basics of animal husbandry, and how to fell timber. William taught him the names and uses and idiosyncrasies of all the different types of trees on the property. By his mid-teens, Bill was already an expert timber cutter, with the physique to match. For her part, Sarah ensured that Bill learned his manners and his alphabet; when he was old enough, Bill made the hour-long journey by foot or on horseback to the little school at Maudsland. The photograph of the group of schoolchildren in their Sunday best which had so fascinated me as a child was in fact the Bignells and children from the other neighbouring farms at the Maudsland school, taken in May 1912. Bill soon grew into a strong and handsome, yet gentle young man, the sort of chap who would cause groups of young girls to giggle and blush and nudge each other as he drove past at the reins of his father's wagon. There was no doubt – Bill Campbell was a bit of a charmer.

In May 1910, just a few months after his eighteenth birthday, Bill began to notice a change in his mother. Sarah seemed to grow tired more quickly, and the heat appeared to bother her more than usual, despite the approach of cooler weather and what passed for winter in those parts. William and Bill grew increasingly worried as Sarah became quiet and withdrawn, but fearing "women's troubles", they did not question her too closely. Sarah struggled on with her daily chores and made no complaint, but with the arrival of spring, it was evident to all that she was losing weight. Around Christmas 1910, Sarah began to complain of pain in her lower back and kidneys, and her swollen eyes watered constantly. As 1910 became 1911, Sarah noticed a swelling in her neck which slowly grew and spread so that she could barely move her chin up and down or turn her head. Listless and in pain, Sarah reluctantly took to her bed.

At the end of April 1911, as Australia and the rest of the British Empire prepared to celebrate the Coronation of King George V and Queen Mary, stricken with worry, William and Bill transported Sarah by horse and cart to the little cottage hospital by the sea at Southport. Upon arrival, she was delivered into the care of the family physician Dr. Brady, who had visited Sarah at the farm a few months previously.

Her body and face were swollen; suffering from goitre due to hyperthyroidism, she was in agony from the resultant chronic kidney infection. Nothing more could be done for her.

Sarah died on Friday 19th May 1911.

She was forty-seven.

14

Topsy

Sarah was buried the very next day in the tiny cemetery at Upper Coomera. William paid for an expensive plot, and a headstone and white-painted iron railings were added a short time afterwards. For how long did he continue to visit? For how long did he continue to place flowers on the grave? Flowers soon fade and become brown and brittle, before turning to dust, dissolved in the rain or blown away by the winds. Perhaps he preferred not to visit at all, and kept alive the memory of how Sarah used to be – the headstrong, independent County Durham lass he fell in love with in a busy Brisbane street.

Certainly, by the time that Edie and her mother received the photograph of the grave, perhaps a few years later, it was shabby, overgrown and uncared for. William would have passed the little cemetery almost every day as he made his deliveries on the wagon and collected goods from Siganto's wharf. Maybe he paused for a few moments at the graveside now and then.

"Hello Sarah, old girl."

I wondered about Margaret Marshall's reaction when she received the letter from William in the summer of 1911, at the height of the Coronation celebrations in Seaham, informing her that another of her daughters was dead. Did she weep for her? Perhaps Margaret had done her grieving for Sarah all those years before as she waved goodbye to her at Durham station. Amongst Edie's possessions in her little attaché case is a tiny Coronation locket in a delicate brass casing, bearing the portrait of King George V on one side, and his wife Queen Mary on the other, which belonged to Edie's mother Fanny. Perhaps Robert Threadkell had purchased this as a gift for his young wife; it is likely that this locket hung around Fanny's neck whilst she read William's letter and news of her sister's death. Fanny had been just four years old when Sarah had left for Queensland; all she really knew and remembered of her older sister was gleaned from her letters and photographs and her mother's memories.

In many ways Sarah's death should have brought my story to an end; in others, it is just the beginning, for it marks the beginning of the regular correspondence between Bill and his family in Seaham. Without Bill and Edie, and their letters and photographs spanning almost twenty five years, there would be no story to tell. Perhaps it was Bill's way of keeping his mother's memory alive, exchanging letters and pictures with those who had known and loved her.

I thought about William and Bill, struggling on in the little cottage at the foot of the mountain, having to cook and clean for themselves and take on the extra burden of all the chores, on top of trying to make a living out of the farm and the delivery business. For young Bill, however, it was not a case of all work and no play. On one of the nearby farms lived the Bignell family; their eldest daughter, Topsy Bignell, had caught Bill's eye. Perhaps they had grown up together, roaming the fields and forests, exploring the gullies and streams, travelling to school in Maudsland on horseback. Topsy was one of eleven children, a confident, lively, outgoing young lady, with a pretty rounded face and big doe eyes, who loved to be the centre of attention, and who was by all accounts, something of a drama queen. The gentle and unassuming Bill was smitten. On 24th September 1912, just sixteen months after Sarah's death, Bill Campbell married Topsy at St Peter's Church in Southport. Bill was twenty, Topsy was two months short of her seventeenth birthday, and already four months pregnant.

The Bignells were an interesting clan. There are still Bignells in and around Tamborine and Coomera today, and all over New South Wales and Queensland. One of Topsy's great-great-grandfathers was Samuel Kingston, an Irishman from Cork, who was convicted of forgery and transported to Australia "for the term of his natural life". He arrived in the penal colony of Sydney on the *Hooghly* on 22nd April 1825, having endured a dreadful voyage aboard the convict ship of some one hundred and seven days. Amazingly, records of Samuel's arrival in the colony remain – he is described as: *"5 feet and 5 and a 1/4 inches, pale complexion, hazel eyes, grey hair with a scar on top of his forehead."* Samuel was not a young man – he was already in his fifties when he arrived.

After serving seven years of their sentence, some convicts were allowed to make an application for permission for their families to join them. Some applied only to discover that their wives or husbands had disowned them and perhaps even remarried. Many unfortunate souls, particularly those who were illiterate, had no means of communicating with their families back in Britain and never heard from them again. At one time, convict ancestry was considered shameful – the histories of so many families were concealed or just not discussed, or "swept under the carpet". Today, having a convict ancestor is a badge of honour, and those poor desperate felons who were transported are known as "Australian Royalty".

Samuel Kingston's application was successful, and on 14th June 1832, his wife Ann, daughters Amelia, Nancy and Lydia, and son Samuel arrived in Sydney Harbour on the *Southworth*. Ann was considerably younger than her husband, and the pair went on to have more children. Samuel Kingston died at Allyn River, New South Wales, in 1852, at the grand old age of eighty five.

His daughter Amelia Kingston married James Bignell, a farmer originally from Hampshire, just months after arriving in Australia, in October 1832, and the family settled at the Bignell family farm at Bandon Grove, Dungog, in the Hunter Valley in New South Wales. The Bignells were renowned for their huge families – there were literally hundreds of them – James and Amelia had fifteen children, fourteen of whom survived to old age. My research was significantly hampered by the fact that each of these fourteen children themselves went on to have twelve, thirteen, fourteen or even fifteen children, all of whom had very similar names.

James and Amelia's children included Samuel Stanley Bignell (born 1838). Around 1872, with a growing family to feed, Samuel decided to seek his fortunes elsewhere, and made his way up through New South Wales, into Southern Queensland, and to the Coomera and Tamborine Mountain, where he purchased a farm on the banks of the Coomera River. Six of his twelve children were born in Upper Coomera.

His fourth child, Alfred Thomas Bignell born in 1860, was a character. He became very active in the growing communities on Tamborine Mountain and down in Upper Coomera, after following his father north to manage one of John Siganto's dairies. In his younger days in New South Wales, Alf had been a very talented cricketer. In the 1880s, before he was married, Alf had played for Northern Districts in Newcastle and was said to have played against an England touring side, captained by James Lilywhite, top scoring with sixty six. A report in the local newspaper described Alf as:

"A magnificent batsman, fast medium accurate bowler and a superb fieldsman... How easy for him to land the ball over the treetops outside the Oval."

He was later invited to represent Australia against England but tragically his family were able to afford neither his keep nor his fare to Melbourne or Sydney or Adelaide, and his opportunity was lost forever.

In the archives at Southport library, there are numerous

photographs of him and his very large family. He married Amy Alice Gray in 1894, and the couple produced twelve children, of whom Topsy (actually named Amelia May) was the eldest. Ivy, Mary, Rebecca, Ada, Kathleen, Samuel, Alfred, George, Amy, Pearl and Janet followed over the course of the next twenty two years. The photograph of the schoolchildren in their Sunday best taken on 23rd May 1912, which had so captured my imagination as child, shows Ivy, Mary, Ada, Kathleen and Sam, each one marked with an ink cross above their heads, by Topsy.

Alf Bignell was a formidable character – one can only imagine how nervous young Bill Campbell was when he had to explain to Alf that he'd got his eldest daughter pregnant, and sought his permission to marry her. It seems Alf and Bill actually got on quite well – Bill had probably known Alf all his life, and he was welcomed into the large Bignell family. As is so often the way with these things, they all simply made the best of it. There is a photograph at the Tamborine Mountain Museum showing Bill and Alf together at the Upper Coomera Rifle Club in 1922; others show them attending various committee meetings together.

After their marriage in September 1912, Topsy moved into the Campbell farmstead on what was by then known locally as Campbell Mountain, to look after Bill and his father. In February 1913, Bill took his heavily pregnant young wife down the mountain to Nurse Bourke's Home in Souter Street, Southport. On 24th February 1913, Topsy gave birth to William John Campbell, named after his father and grandfather, and known as Willie. She was just seventeen, and her own parents, Alf and Alice, would go on to have three more children, Amy, Pearl and Janet. Another baby soon followed for Bill and Topsy – by the time she was nineteen Topsy was already a mother of two. Elsie Jean (known as Jean) was born on 25th August 1914, just after war had been declared in Europe.

Amongst the photographs in Edie's box are two photographs of Bill and Topsy and their two eldest children. The first shows the young couple on the porch of their cottage, now extended to accommodate their growing family. Bill, moustachioed and in his best clothes, is holding Willie in his arms, whilst Topsy is sitting next to him, her hair pinned up, baby Jean on her lap. Bill looks older than his years; Topsy still looks like a child. In the second photograph, the couple are sitting on the family's cart, pulled by two blinkered horses, Bill in shirtsleeves and a hat, reins in hand. Topsy is wearing her best white hat, baby Jean wrapped in a shawl on her knee, Willie is wriggling around between his parents. You can almost hear Bill muttering "Sit STILL for the man with the camera Willie!". But Willie didn't sit still and all that can be seen is his hat. I have grown to love these two photographs, as I have grown to love the people in them.

By the time of Jean's birth, Mount Tamborine was no longer an isolated community of a few hardy pioneer farmers and timber cutters. The *Beaudesert Times* that year opined:

> "Tamborine Mountain is a different place from what it was a few years ago. About five years ago there were only 5 families at the northern end of Tamborine Mountain. Now there are enough people here to start a dancing club and a tennis club. A picnic was arranged for the opening day Saturday 11th October. There was a good attendance, no less than 48 people being present."

When Britain declared war on Germany on 4th August 1914, Australia, as a dominion of the British Empire, was automatically at war too. Across the Empire, from Seaham Harbour to Nova Scotia, from the Scottish Highlands to the Southern Alps of New Zealand, young men from every village and town waved goodbye to parents, sweethearts and children and sailed to the far side of the world to fight for the motherland, a country most had never set foot in and were unlikely to ever see, in a war that was not of their making. "All over by Christmas", they said. As in Britain, news of the declaration of war was initially greeted with enthusiasm and young men across the nation rushed to enlist.

In 1914 the population of Australia was around five million. Some 416,809 men enlisted, almost ten per cent of the population. Of these, sixty thousand were killed, and another one hundred and fifty-six thousand gassed, wounded or taken prisoner. Most of the Australian troops were sent initially not to Europe but to Egypt, to counter the threat from the Turkish Ottoman Empire which, keen to extend its influence in the Middle East, had formed an alliance with Germany. The Australians together with a large contingent of New Zealanders, and French and British troops, landed at the now-infamous peninsula of Gallipoli on 25th April 1915. Unable to make any significant headway, there they remained for seven long months, under constant attack from Turkish forces, before being evacuated on 19th and 20th December 1915.

After the farce of Gallipoli, the Australian units were reorganised and shipped off to Northern France, where they were deployed in March 1916. With insufficient training, the ANZAC troops were totally unprepared for the horrors of trench warfare. In their first significant engagement at the battle of Fromelles, the Australians suffered five thousand, five hundred and fifty-three casualties in the first twenty-four hours. By the end of 1916, just five months later, forty thousand had been killed or injured. The following year, there were a further seventy-eight thousand casualties as the Australians fought at Bullecourt, Messines and Passchendaele. However, it was not only upon the battlefields of France and Belgium that Australian lives were lost; some units were deployed in the Desert Campaign, defending the Suez Canal, recapturing the Sinai Desert, before eventually pushing on to "liberate" Palestine, Lebanon and Syria.

The massive casualty rate was not sustainable, and began to cause tensions back in Australia as popular support for the war began to waiver and political divisions began to emerge. Families and businesses across the nation began to feel the financial implications as they lost breadwinners and employees. As in Britain, Australian women had to step in to take over the jobs of the menfolk serving overseas. Losses were so significant that the Australian government wanted to introduce conscription. Referenda were held in 1916 and 1917; the country was divided, resulting in civil disturbances and riots. Even amongst the citizens of Mount Tamborine there was discord. On each occasion, the majority of Queenslanders voted against conscription, but feelings ran high. In 1917 a fight broke out down at Upper Coomera between two families of opposing views. The situation quickly got out of hand and the police were brought in who eventually broke up the fighting, but not before reading the Riot Act.[58]

How remote from the theatre of war ten thousand miles away were the little communities on Tamborine Mountain and Upper Coomera, and yet still the Great War cast its shadow. Many of the district's young men had volunteered when war broke out. Ernie Jenyns and Frank Curtis were killed in action, along with Topsy's cousin Sid Bignell, who died at Bouzencourt, in the Somme, on 10th April 1918, just seven months before the armistice, aged twenty-five. The fiancée of Topsy's younger sister Ivy, Douglas Hollindale, who grew up on the farm next door to the Campbells, was gassed whilst fighting in France. Douglas was one of the lucky ones – he survived his injuries, returning to the mountain after the war, and he and Ivy were married shortly afterwards.

The mountain villagers held numerous fundraising events throughout the course of the war, while the local women knitted hundreds of sets of hats and socks and gloves to be sent out to France. The Bignells and the Campbells helped organise some of the fundraisers, one of which is recorded in the *Beaudesert Times* newspaper:

---

58 *The Turning Years – A Tamborine Mountain History*, Eve Curtis, North Tamborine, 1988, p. 70.

"On Saturday 19th October 1918, a most successful picnic was held in the grounds of 'Wilmont' in aid of the War Nurses Fund. The grounds were gay with flags, the Union Jack and the Australian Flag floating on either side of the entrance gate. Games and sport for the young folk passed the time most pleasantly ... refreshments were provided by the ladies of the south end of the mountain in their usual generous manner. In the evening a dance was held, Mr A T Bignell [Alf] kindly leading the room which was beautifully decorated with ferns, zamia palms and flags, by Mrs W Campbell [Topsy] of Guanaba, assisted by Mrs F Young of the mountain."[59]

Topsy was in her element when she was entertaining and playing the role of hostess; however, her ambitions in this area would ultimately have heartrending implications for the Campbells. At the Armistice, Bill and Topsy were parents to three small children, a second daughter Kathleen Mary having been born in January 1917. A third girl Irene Sarah (named after the grandmother she never knew, but always known as Betty) was born in September 1919, followed by another boy, Alfred James (Jimmy), born in October 1921. By the time she was twenty-seven, Topsy was a mother of six children under nine years old. As the eldest of twelve children herself, some of whom were younger than her own, Topsy was unphased. Unlike Sarah Campbell, Topsy had her mother, father, sisters, numerous aunts, uncles and cousins to call upon for assistance. Sarah had had no one.

Remarkably, despite the demands of six small children, fulfilling the role of a farmer's wife and looking after Bill and his now ageing father William senior, Topsy took over the family letter-writing duties and struck up a friendship through correspondence with her husband's family back in County Durham. Perhaps she was keen to ensure that Bill maintained his links with his late mother's family. So many of the photographs

---

59 *Beaudesert Times*, 1ˢᵗ November 1918, cited ibid.

that were sent across the miles to little Edie and her mother back in Seaham Harbour bear Topsy's handwriting and sometimes child-like descriptions on the back; sadly, not one of the letters which accompanied the photographs survives.

15

On Caroline Street

In the twenty five years since Sarah Marshall had left Seaham for Queensland, the little town had changed significantly. By the time Fanny Threadkell received the news of her sister's death in early summer 1911, the combined villages of Seaham Harbour and New Seaham (formerly Seaham Colliery) were home to some fifteen thousand people – miners mostly, from Seaham Colliery but also Dawdon pit, which had opened in 1899. There were also railwaymen, seamen, bottle workers, fishermen and labourers, as well as members of the "professional classes" – teachers, doctors, solicitors, ship owners and shipping agents, and colliery managers, and an army of tradespeople and merchants of various sorts. The basic terraced cottages, hastily built to accommodate the town's influx of workers in the 1850s and 1860s, were no longer sufficient to house the population; overcrowding and squalor were rife.

The ramshackle lanes and back streets which had grown up around the harbour area were in many cases unfit for human habitation, but were crammed with the poorest of the town's residents and their broods of children. Summersons Buildings (where my grandfather was born in 1917), Hunters Buildings, the bottom end of Frances Street nearest to the docks, and the streets around the railway and behind North Road were, in places, nothing better than slums interspersed with rough drinking establishments. The further away from the harbour area, by and large, the better the accommodation became.

Fanny and Robert Threadkell lived in number 6 Caroline Street, the more "respectable" end of Seaham Harbour, just around the corner from St John's Church and the National School, which Edie would start attending in September of that year, and opposite the Methodist Church. They had originally lived in 55 Frances Street, just after their marriage, and Edie was born there. None of the original buildings of Caroline Street survive. The only reminder of its existence is the street name itself, carved into the stonework on the side of a building at the top of Church Street, currently a furnishings store. Caroline Street, and Frances Street which joined at a ninety degree angle and ran down parallel to the back of Church Street, were built in around 1865. Halfway down Frances Street there was a public house, the Volunteer Arms. It's still there, a solitary and seemingly incongruous reminder of days gone by, and of a street of homes long since vanished. After years of standing derelict, it is about to re-open as a smart new café.

The tiny terraced houses in Caroline Street consisted of a single room downstairs, with a door straight in off the street. There was a kitchen range, a window at either end of the room, a large table in the centre of the room and a pantry next to the back door, which opened out onto a shared yard. Upstairs there was one bedroom and a tiny box room above the stairs. The back yard was shared between the families who occupied 5, 6, 7 and 8 Caroline Street and the two families who lived above 8 Frances Street on the corner. In the yard there was a sink, two toilets (shared between six families) and a laundry, together with a couple of coal houses. There was no running water or toilets in any of the houses, and no bathrooms. Bathing was done in a tin bath that hung by the side of the kitchen range until required, or at the public baths. A washstand with a jug and a basin stood in the bedroom. By modern standards this sounds a quite appalling way to exist; in 1911, it was the norm. Millions of families up and down the country lived in exactly the same way.

Robert Threadkell was rarely at home for any length of time, as he was often away at sea. At the time of the 1911 census, carried out in April, Fanny is described as "head of the household" and there is no trace of Robert elsewhere in the census records. Presumably he was on one of his sea voyages.

Despite the lack of decent housing in the town, large amounts of money were spent by the authorities and by private investors on leisure facilities for the masses. The 6th Marquess of Londonderry had donated ninety-five acres of land near Dawdon for the creation of a golf club, which was formally opened on 15th May 1911. The Boy Scout movement was in its infancy, and the Seaham and District Scout Association was formed in August 1911, followed two years later by the Girl Guides. Headed by the formidable Miss Dillon, the Girl Guides met in a hut constructed in the gardens of Dene House. Edie was one of Seaham's earliest Girl Guides, joining just after her tenth birthday in 1916, and she remained a great supporter of the organisation throughout her life.

Seaham's first cinema, the Empire, was opened in 1912, along with a new theatre, the Princess, on Princess Road. The burgeoning population required new schools, so the Upper Standard School was opened in Princess Road the same year, as was Byron Terrace, to accommodate children from New Seaham and Seaton. Byron Terrace School is still going strong, and is today a popular and high-achieving primary school.

Much excitement was caused in the town on Monday 25th August 1913 when crowds of onlookers gathered on Seaham beach for their first glimpse of an aeroplane. A Sopwith Biplane piloted by Harry Hawker, which was competing in the Circuit of Britain Air Race, made an unscheduled landing at Seaham for urgent repairs. Such was the hazardous nature of aviation at the time that of the four entrants in the race, only Hawker's aircraft actually took off; his passenger, Harry Kauper, had been rendered unconscious by carbon monoxide fumes on the first attempt at the race a week previously. Of the other entrants, one pilot was killed during testing, another aircraft had been damaged during trials and the third suffered engine failure just prior to take off. Thousands of Seaham folk flocked to the beach just near to the Featherbed Rock to see the brave airmen and their amazing machine, and watched as the little plane took off for its next destination, Beadnell in Northumberland. Hawker and Kauper never did complete the Circuit – they got as far as Dublin, but as they were the only competitors they were awarded the huge £1000 prize anyway.

All was not well in Seaham. The relationship between the miners and their unions on the one hand, and the colliery owners on the other, remained fractious at best. Since the days following the explosion of September 1880, the miners' unions had grown in strength and in membership, and were a political force to be reckoned with. In 1872, the Durham Miners Association had thirty-one thousand members; by 1910 this had grown to almost one hundred and thirty-two thousand. It is difficult to comprehend the size and importance of the mining industry in Britain at that time. At its peak in 1913, there were three hundred and four pits employing over one hundred and sixty-five thousand men in County Durham (which then included Sunderland, South Shields and Gateshead) alone.[60] Though much had been achieved in terms of workers' rights, particularly in respect of pay and conditions, there was still much to do. Coal mining remained an extremely arduous and hazardous occupation; accidents and fatalities remained commonplace.

In the days before the nationalisation of the coal industry, wages and conditions varied hugely, not only from county to county, but even at local level, from colliery to colliery. The Labour Party had been formed in 1906 and the Durham Miners Association joined with the largest of the miners' unions, the Mining Federation of Great Britain, which had allied itself with the Party in 1908. By 1912, a wave of social, political and

---

60   The Growth and Expansion of the Durham Miners' Association (Part 2), Raymond Chesterfield, www.durhamintime.org.uk

industrial unrest swept Britain, accompanied by much talk of revolution.[61] This turbulent period in British history is largely overlooked today, overshadowed by the horrors of the Great War.

The miners held the trump card – they could, and did, frequently hold the government to ransom. In a time when coal was the very lifeblood of this great industrial nation, strike action for any significant length of time would paralyse the country. Once the stockpiles had been exhausted, locomotives would stand idle in their sidings. Ports and harbours would be crammed with steamships, the warehouses overflowing with cargo that wasn't going anywhere. Factories would have to cease production – no coal meant no power. Within days Britain would grind to a halt, as the miners enjoyed support from their comrades in the docks and on the railways. The miners knew it. The government knew it.

The miners had three main demands: a national minimum wage, a national agreement, so that all negotiations could be dealt with at a nationwide rather than local level, and nationalisation of the industry as a whole. Strike committees were formed at Seaham and Dawdon collieries, a pattern replicated at every colliery across the nation. The Durham miners voted 57,490 for strike action, 28,504 against.[62] On 1st March 1912, eight hundred thousand miners came out on strike, marking the biggest strike Britain had ever seen. Soon a million men were out. The government was forced to intervene and brokered a compromise, and by the end of April, all the miners were back at work. Although the pitmen had achieved their aim of a national minimum wage, the government went back on its word. Deceived by the empty promises of politicians, the miners' leaders now began to fight in earnest for the cause of nationalisation. In

---

61 'Black Friday 1921', Patrick Renshaw, *History Today* Vol.21 issue 6 June 1971, reproduced at www.historytoday.com/patrick-renshaw/black-friday-1921

62 The Growth and Expansion of the Durham Miners' Association (Part 2), Raymond Chesterfield, www.durhamintime.org.uk

1913 the Triple Alliance was formed, when the miners' union joined forces with the National Union of Railwaymen and the National Transport Workers' Federation. The "Class War" may have begun but it would be stopped in its tracks by the events of the summer of 1914.

A German merchant ship, *Comet,* was docked in Seaham Harbour on the day that war broke out; the unfortunate crew were immediately arrested, ordered off the ship and then marched up Church Street, escorted by police officers and members of the local Volunteer Force to the police station on the corner of Tempest Road. There is a photograph of these poor sailors, all civilians, who had done nothing wrong other than to be of the wrong nationality in the wrong place at the wrong time, walking up Church Street past jeering crowds of the town's residents.

As on Tamborine Mountain and across the Empire, the young men of Seaham flocked to enlist as soon as war was declared. To many of them, who had never been further than perhaps Durham or Sunderland or South Shields, it was all a bit of lark, a chance to see more of the world. Among the archives there is a "Roll of Honour", which lists those of the Marquis of Londonderry's employees who served: one thousand and eighty seven from Seaham Colliery (including John Clyde, my great-grandfather), seven hundred and twenty three from Dawdon Colliery, thirteen from the Londonderry Offices, twenty-four estate workers from Seaham Hall, twelve from the Engine Works, and another ten from the Wagon Works. This pattern was replicated in every trade, from the bottle works to the Co-Op – every factory, every parish and every colliery had its own roll of honour, and later, its own memorial.

Of the thousands of Seaham men and boys who answered the call, some six hundred and forty-eight did not return. Many were enlisted in the famous Durham regiment, the Durham Light Infantry (DLI) which had been formed in 1881 from an amalgamation of other Durham Regiments. In Durham

Cathedral, just a few paces from the Miners' Memorial, you will find the DLI chapel, where the walls are inscribed with the regiment's most famous battles, Salamanca, Inkerman, Sebastopol, New Zealand, Ladysmith, Ypres, Loos, Somme, Dunkirk, Tobruk and El Alamein amongst them. The ragged, threadbare standards from long-forgotten military campaigns now hang overhead, faded reminders of a once mighty Empire and the men who fought to create and preserve it. A detachment from the 4th Battalion of the Light Infantry was stationed at Seaham, on coastal defence duties, but most men were sent to France in 1915.

The Roll of Honour at New Seaham Working Men's Club is filled with names still familiar in the town – Scollens, McGanns, Currys, McCabes, Tempests, Curwens, Vickers, Bagleys, Cardys, Guys, and Deftys. Seaham Hall, along with Vane House and other large properties in the town, was taken over by the 28th Durham Voluntary Aid Detachment for use as a military hospital, treating over three and half thousand injured servicemen throughout the course of the war. Other buildings were commandeered for stores, officers' quarters, billets and canteens.

With so many of the town's men enlisting, there was always work to be found at the mines; there was a shortage of skilled labour within the mining industry across the country as a whole, due to the vast numbers of men being lost to the war effort. Eventually drastic measures had to be introduced by the government to keep the country's coal mines operating; some of those who enlisted were sent not to France to fight but down into the pits. Many of these young men had no experience or knowledge of the mining industry, and once again the number of accidents and fatalities began to increase.

Edie Threadkell was a month shy of her eighth birthday when war was declared. Her father Robert was sixty-one, relatively elderly by the standards of the day (the average male life expectancy was still in the low fifties) but still a mariner.

In the days before state pension, you worked until you could work no longer, until you died or if you were lucky, had some savings or adult children to support you through your dotage. Robert had been at sea for half a century, since he was a boy. He had witnessed the death of the age of sail and the dawn of the age of steam and he had no intention of allowing the outbreak of war to confine him to shore. Although Edie and Fanny did not notice any difference in terms of the amount of time Robert spent away at sea during the war years, Robert's safety was no longer threatened just by harsh weather and high seas; the ships of the British Merchant Marine were now legitimate targets for the ultimate new weapon of the German Navy, the U-Boat.

The merchant vessels and colliers that transported coal from the north-east pits to London and the major ports were under almost constant attack. Many were torpedoed and sunk, with great loss of life, including ships belonging to the Londonderry fleet, carrying coal from the Marquis' County Durham collieries from Seaham Harbour. The trawler *Helvetia* was sunk in 1916, and the cargo vessel *Vianna* was lost in 1918 – its wreck still lies four miles east off the Seaham coast. One of the boats carrying bottles from John Candlish's glass works hit a mine in 1917 and exploded, with the loss of four lives. The *Lady Londonderry* was sunk in the Thames Estuary, and the *Lord Stewart* and *Lady Helen* were torpedoed. Another of the Londonderry fleet, the *SS Stewart's Court* was torpedoed within sight of Seaham. Thirteen of her crew were saved by the Seaham lifeboat, the *Elliot Galer*.[63] The German U-Boats wrought havoc up and down the eastern coast of England, but it wasn't just shipping that was targeted – they also possessed the capability to attack targets on land, as the residents of Seaham Colliery found to their cost.

On the evening of 11th July 1916, New Seaham (as Seaham Colliery had now become known) was shelled by a German U-Boat, the infamous UB39. An estimated thirty-nine shells fell in the fields around Dalton-le-Dale and Mount Pleasant, and

63   Seaham Timeline, www.east-durham.co.uk

around the Mill Inn, but some hit the village directly, fatally injuring Mrs Mary Slaughter as she walked through the pit yard with her friend. At 14 Doctor Street, the home of Danish miner Carl Mortenson and his family, a shell came straight through the back wall, through the kitchen where Mrs Mortenson was standing, and landed by the front door; miraculously the shell failed to detonate, and the Mortenson family, including the children sleeping upstairs, were saved. All escaped injury.[64]

A photograph still exists of the crew of UB39 standing next to the guns on the deck, grinning at the camera. This photograph was taken on 12th July 1916, the day after the attack on Seaham, and appears in the memoirs of UB39's captain, Werner Fuerbringer. Known as FIPS, Fuerbringer was one of the German Navy's greatest U-boat commanders. He had joined the German Navy as a cadet in 1901; by the end of the war, in 1918, he had sunk one hundred and two merchant ships and was awarded the Iron Cross, the highest German military honour. He continued to serve though World War Two, achieving the rank of Konteradmiral, finally retiring in 1943.[65] In his memoirs, published in 1933, he describes in detail the attack on Seaham – he thought he was raining shells upon the ironworks. *"I was assuming that the factory would have only a skeleton staff on the premises at night."* he recalled. *"My objective was the destruction of war materials and not people."*[66] In fact, he had of course targeted the pit, a mile or so inland.

Robert Threadkell finally retired at the end of the war, worn out by a cold, brutal and perilous life at sea. The only record of his war service which still exists is a note card recording the issuing of his medals in 1919. Those medals are still in their tiny buff cardboard packets, and kept in the rough wooden box that

---

64   Durham at War, www.durhamatwar.org.uk

65   www.uboat.net/wwi/commanders/81.html

66   FIPS, Legendary U Boat Commander 1915–1918, translated by G. Brooks, 2000. Originally published in Berlin, 1933, under the title *"Alarm! Tauchen! U-Boot in Kampf und Sturm"*, contributed to www. durhamatwar.org.uk by Durham County Record Office.

Robert himself had made to while away the hours on a long sea voyage. For the first time since his early teens, he spent every day at home, in the little house in Caroline Street, with Fanny and Edie, where his older children from his first marriage would call to visit with his grandchildren. And every day he would walk down Frances Street, perhaps calling in at the Volunteer Arms for a pint and a smoke; drawn towards the docks, he would lean upon the railings and watch the tugs and pilots guide vessels of all sizes in and out of the harbour, past the little black and white lighthouse.

Throughout the course of the war, amid the chaos and the hardships and the quiet desperation, every six months or so, a small brown envelope would arrive on the doormat of 6 Caroline Street, bearing an Australian postage stamp and Topsy Campbell's unmistakable handwriting, bringing news and photographs from Tamborine Mountain and Upper Coomera. How Fanny and little Edie must have looked forward to these letters arriving; perhaps they spent many a long winter night together when Robert was at sea writing letters and drawing pictures, sorting newspaper clippings and photographs to be sent out to Queensland. And every few months, as he made his daily rounds with his horse and delivery wagon, William Campbell would pick up from the little post office at Upper Coomera a small brown envelope addressed to "Mr & Mrs W J Campbell, Guanaba, Upper Coomera, Queensland, Australia". He would automatically begin to peel open the envelope and then he would remember, and stuff the letter back into his pocket.

16

The Turn of the Screw

Any sense of optimism the people of Seaham and Seaton had possessed at the end of the war very soon diminished. The feelings of patriotism and euphoria did not last long, as the men who had fought in France and Belgium returned home, jaded and perhaps with a different view of the world. Gradually they resumed their ordinary jobs and occupations, in the coal mines, on the railways, in the docks, in the bottle works, and renewed their old battles against their employers. The Coalition government had taken control of the mining industry in 1917, at the height of the hostilities in Europe, and the miners leaders had hoped that this would be the first step towards nationalisation.

Although the Londonderrys were still very much the "Lords of Seaham", the death of the 6th Marquess in 1915 marked the beginning of the end of that family's relationship with the town they had created. The new Death Duties Tax, or inheritance tax as we know it, crippled the Londonderrys and their fortunes began to wane. Many of the family's assets and lands were sold off and they moved out of Seaham Hall completely.[67] The Hall was offered up for auction by the 7th Marquis in 1922, but nobody wanted it, and this once grand dwelling which had hosted the cream of British high society began to fall into disrepair. The beautiful terraced gardens, once tended by a small army of gardeners, soon became overgrown with weeds and ivy; the white stucco walls shabby and peeling, the ballroom and

---

67 www.durhamrecordsonline.com/literature

grand salons damp and dusty. Seaham Hall was, quite simply, abandoned.

Britain was on the brink of ruin after the war, and there was much talk in government of wage reductions as the industrialised world began to slip into recession. The government had retained control of the coal industry even after the war had ended, but were unwilling to force wage cuts on the miners in fear of strike action and political instability. The colliery owners had wrongly assumed that the economy would go into overdrive once the war was over, and were anxious to regain control. However, after a brief boom around 1919/20, coal exports actually began to fall quite dramatically in early 1921, and Lloyd George's government couldn't return the industry to the hands of its private owners quickly enough. Unemployment rates in mining communities went through the roof as miners across the country were laid off, and between three hundred thousand and four hundred thousand miners found themselves out of work with no income.[68]

The nation's collieries were returned to private ownership at the end of March 1921. The miners were devastated – nationalisation, which had seemed so close and an inevitability at the end of the war, was now further away than ever, and the mine owners responded to the tumbling coal prices in the only manner they knew – by implementing savage wage cuts, of up to forty-nine per cent in areas of South Wales,[69] and planning to return to the old system of district rates, in contravention of the national wage agreements which had been reached before the war. The Miners' Union leaders suggested a pool system by introducing a levy on every ton of coal produced, so that the high output collieries could in effect subsidise those with poor outputs; the mine owners opposed the pool system as anti-competitive, even if it meant the less profitable collieries being

68   "Black Friday 1921", Patrick Renshaw, *History Today* Vol.21 issue 6 June 1971, reproduced at www.historytoday.com/patrick-renshaw/black-friday-1921.

69   Ibid, p. 4.

abandoned and massive unemployment. It seemed that little had changed since the Londonderrys had stopped up the seams where the bodies of their employees lay so that production could resume after the 1880 explosion at Seaham Colliery. Profit before people.

Unsurprisingly the miners rejected the owners' new terms and conditions – from 1st April, 1921 any man who opposed his employer found himself "locked out" and unable to work. The dockers and the railway unions called a strike to support the miners, scheduled to start on 15th April. The government faced the very real possibility that two million men would be out on strike and the country would grind to a halt. Nationally, there was already a similar number of workers unemployed. With an eye on recent events in Russia, and fearing they would have a revolution on their hands, the government response was brutal and threatening. When negotiations between the miners' leaders and Lloyd George's cabinet broke down, a state of emergency was called, eighty thousand special constables were called up, and most disturbingly of all, machine gun posts were put in place at some collieries.[70] The class war was threatening to become so much more than an ideological battle, ramped up by apocalyptic rhetoric on both sides.

In a speech to the House of Commons, the Prime Minister warned that:

"The nation is, for the first time in its history, confronted by an attempt to coerce it into capitulation by the destruction of its resources, and this menace is apparently now to be supplemented by a concerted plan to suspend the transport services which are essential to the life of the country…"

Behind the scenes however, Lloyd George was trying to achieve a settlement, but negotiations were undermined by divisions in

70   Ibid, p. 5.

the miners ranks and, at the eleventh hour, on 21st April, 1921, a day remembered as "Black Friday", the railway union leaders withdrew their support for the strike and, much to the relief of the government, the Triple Alliance of miners, dockers and railway workers unions was at an end.

The miners fought until July 1921, when they were forced back to work through pure financial desperation, on terms even more savage than those on offer prior to Black Friday. The average pay for a miner fell from eighty-nine shillings and eight pence a week to fifty-eight shillings and ten pence.[71] The miners faced brutal criticism from all quarters, and were rapidly losing public sympathy. An article published in The Spectator on 1st July 1921, captured the mood of the time:

> "The miners, so far as their wages are concerned, have remained idle for 3 months to no purpose. They are poorer by 3 months' pay, and have gained nothing... The long strike has been a fresh proof of the futility and wickedness of great strikes...many of the miners will find that they have destroyed their own sources of employment. A number of mines are permanently flooded and abandoned...the miners have incurred the ill-will of their fellow workmen by their manifest selfishness."[72]

For the miners of Seaham, the fight was to last for another seventy years. For some, it never ends.

Immediately after the strike ended in July 1921, and just a few months before Edie Threadkell's fifteenth birthday, a young couple, John and Lydia Clyde, moved into the empty property next door at 7 Caroline Street, with their six month old daughter, also called Lydia. John was a miner at Seaham Colliery, where he had worked from the age of twelve; in 1915,

---

71   Ibid, p. 10.
72   The End of the Miners' Strike, The Spectator, 1st July 1921, p. 12, www. archive.spectator.co.uk

he had enlisted in the army with his mates and his brother Sep, and was sent to northern France with the Light Infantry where he had served as a medical orderly and stretcher-bearer on the battlefields. John and Lydia were my great-grandparents, young Lydia my grandmother. I can still remember being shown by my grandmother, when I was very small, how to wind and apply bandages, as it was done in the field, just like John had taught her. Fanny, Robert and Edie took an immediate shine to the young Clyde family, and so began a close friendship between the two families that would last for generations, and which would ultimately result in Edie's battered little case of photographs and letters coming into my possession.

Another child, a boy, Jack, was born to the Clydes in 1923, and he was always Edie's favourite.

The 1920s and 1930s were hard, desperate times in Seaham and Seaton, as they were in many mining and heavy industrial communities throughout the country. For some, there seemed no way out of the grinding poverty and suicide rates in the town went through the roof. Between 1920 and 1937 it is estimated that over twenty residents took their own lives – some by hanging or other violent means, but most simply by just walking into the sea or throwing themselves from the pier. Just as the miners' strike was ending, John Candlish's bottle works shut down. The closure of the Londonderry Engine Works in Foundry Road followed shortly afterwards in 1924.

Perhaps to remind his employees of the power his family had over their lives and to emphasise their authority, the 7th Marquis had a statue of his father, the 6th Marquis, erected outside the company offices at the south end of Terrace Green in 1922. It's still there, opposite the cafes, estate agents and shops on North Terrace. The Londonderrys, their fortunes and interest in Seaham fading somewhat, decided to try to boost their coffers by sinking a third mine on the cliff tops within sight of Seaham Hall. Named Vane-Tempest after the famous Frances Anne Vane Tempest Stewart, Marchioness of Londonderry, the first sod for the sinking of the shaft was cut in 1923. By 1929 the first coals were being produced, bringing desperately needed employment to Seaham's townsfolk. This was to be the last survivor of the town's great mines, finally closing in 1992. Today, there's no sign it was ever there. If you reside in the affluent housing estate of East Shore Village, you are actually living right in the middle of what was the Vane Tempest pit yard. The Londonderry family had very little personal involvement with the town they had created after the sinking of their newest colliery, and were very infrequent visitors to Seaham.

The Threadkells weren't wealthy by any stretch of the imagination, but nor were they poor. Robert had looked after his finances very well during his years at sea; supplemented by Edie's income from various menial jobs, the family "got by" throughout the economic decline of the 1920s. My mother recalls that they always had high quality, quite expensive furniture, and "nice" things in the house. In those days, the sense of community was strong, and neighbours looked after each other and so it was with the Threadkells and the Clydes. North-east mining folk of the day may have looked, spoken and indeed behaved roughly, but beneath the coal dust there were (and still are) golden hearts.

The Clydes found themselves in desperate need of good neighbours in 1926, as once again the town's miners came out on strike. The first Labour government, lead by Ramsay Macdonald, had been elected in 1924 but survived for only nine months. With the Conservatives, led by Stanley Baldwin back in power, at the end of June 1925 the colliery owners had announced an end to all national agreements and abolished the minimum wage; in many collieries, workers who refused to accept this were once again locked out. In May 1926, the General Council of the Trades Union Congress called a strike in support of over a million miners who had been locked out for failing to agree to the 1925 wage reductions. For ten days, one million seven hundred thousand British workers in all areas of transport and heavy industry – dockyards, gas works, shipyards, construction, engineering, railways – came out on strike. However, many within the TUC and the Labour Party had concerns that the strike would be hijacked by communists and revolutionaries, and support for the strike began to waiver within days. The government had been planning for a general strike for almost a year, and had plans in place to keep the country moving. There is every chance that, had Winston Churchill (then Chancellor of the Exchequer) got his way and placed armed troops at picket lines, the country could have descended into disaster. A Court ruling against one of the unions involved declared the strike illegal, and participating unions faced having their assets seized by employers. The TUC called off the strike on 12th May 1926.

The miners stayed out. In a development that was incredibly unusual for the time, even King George expressed his sympathy with the strikers, famously warning, *"Try living on their wages before you judge them."* Throughout the summer 1926, the miners stayed out, experiencing unimaginable hardships, many on the brink of starvation, supported only by the charity of good neighbours and church organisations who established soup kitchens to help feed the starving families. Neighbours like the Threadkells who weren't on strike would "make an extra bit of dinner" if they could afford it, and take it next door where it would be gratefully accepted. As winter approached, many families resorted to burning their furniture or stealing coal to keep warm. Gradually, worn down by the grinding poverty, miners in other parts of the country began to return to work, but the Durham miners stayed out until the end of November, a month longer than any other coalfield.[73] For seven long months, the men of Seaham and the surrounding areas stood firm but faced with a bitter winter without income, food and fuel, eventually they accepted the Union instruction to return to work, and returned to work on 30th November 1926. It should be noted that some of the colliery owners provided meals in

---

73   The Growth and Expansion of the Durham Miners' Association (Part 2), Raymond Chesterfield, www.durhamintime.org.uk

schools, and declined to evict the miners who were unable to pay rent from their tied cottages. Whether they were motivated by benevolence or the fear of riot remains to be seen. Such was the impact of the strike upon the little community, my grandmother, Lydia, would often talk about it. She was just five and a half years old at the time, but the strike and its aftermath left an indelible mark upon her childhood.

By the end of the strike, Edie was a young woman of twenty. Jobs were incredibly hard to come by, for both men and women, and she took a job as an attendant at the ladies' rest rooms behind St John's Church at the top of Church Street and the back of Marlborough Street. The restrooms were housed in a one storey building, and as well as housing the ladies' public conveniences, they contained a sitting area with polished wood benches, and opened out onto a small garden. For over forty years Edie looked after the ladies' rest rooms, and kept them immaculately clean and tidy, and she lovingly maintained the little garden. Everybody in Seaham Harbour knew Edie Threadkell, and Edie Threadkell knew everybody else. She also got to hear about everything that went on in the town, from the gossiping women who visited her little domain.

Although the Durham miners garnered some optimism from the Labour Party gains in the 1929 General Election, and the election of Ramsay MacDonald as MP for Seaham Harbour, Labour did not have enough seats for an overall majority and were forced into coalition with the Liberals. Seaham suddenly found itself at the centre of British politics, but this did little to ameliorate the situation of its townspeople. Any hopes that their situation might be improved under Ramsay MacDonald's government were quickly dashed when the economies of the industrialised nations were plunged into steep recession by the Wall Street Crash, when the American stock market collapsed. The effect of the Great Depression was brutal and immediate. Coal mines were shut down across the country, creating one hundred per cent unemployment in some small towns and villages, and the number of miners in Durham fell by around sixty-five thousand from 1924 to 1931.[74]

By mid-1931, unemployment nationally was around two and a half million. MacDonald put forward proposals for savage cuts in public spending and lost the support of many of his own senior ministers; he resigned in August 1931 and was asked by the King to form a National Government of all three parties, in an attempt to deal with the crisis. He did so but was expelled from the Labour Party for his pains, set up his own party, and would become a reviled figure in Labour politics for decades. Increasingly side-lined by poor physical and mental health, he resigned the role of Prime Minister in 1935, and lost his Seaham Harbour seat to Labour's Emmanuel Shinwell in the 1935 election.

As things went from bad to worse for the people of Seaham and Seaton, Edie faced her own trials. On 25th July 1930, after a short illness, Robert Threadkell passed away, aged seventy seven. In Edie's box, underneath the letters and photographs sent by Bill and Topsy Campbell, lies Robert Threadkell's will, and the Grant of Probate to his Executors. Robert left his estate of £201 2s 10d (around £11,700 today) to Fanny, after providing legacies of £5 to each of his daughters from his first marriage, and to Edie.

Despite the dire economic situation and the straitened circumstances of the miners and their families, Seaham was changing. In 1926, when the town was at its lowest ebb, construction began of a large new housing estate at Carr House Farm (later known as Deneside) designed to provide homes for some of the town's poorest residents in anticipation of slum clearance around the railway line and the bottom of Church Street.

The first mains electricity arrived in the town in 1927, and new schools opened in Camden Square, Princess Road and Low Colliery. The town began to take on a form much more familiar

---

74   Ibid.

to its current residents, and by 1936 over three thousand people had been rehoused.

Even Seaton Village was changing. By 1938 the tiny village school closed its doors and said goodbye to its very last pupil, Adamson Raffle. In the same year, the ancient little square of ten cottages and farmhouse that had sat opposite the Village Farmhouse for centuries, with their outside staircases and courtyard well, which Sarah would have known so well from her time in the village, were demolished. All that remains is the front step of one of the cottages, now the stile which leads to the Dun Cow field.

17

The Gunalda Hotel

While the folk of Seaham were enduring unprecedented hardships, on the other side of the world, on the farm at the foot of Tamborine Mountain, Bill and Topsy Campbell were also struggling to make ends meet. Severe droughts in 1919, 1922 and 1923 affected the Coomera region badly, and were followed by floods in 1924 and 1925. Further drought in 1927 and more seemingly endless rain in 1927 and 1928 rendered farming an increasingly difficult way to make a living. Drought, flood, drought, flood. That's always been the way in Southern Queensland. It still is.

The Campbell family had grown too – a fifth child, Jimmy, was born in 1921. Life was hard, especially for Topsy, caring for five small children, as well as the men of the house, Bill and William senior. All eight of them were crammed together in the little slab cottage that William had built thirty years before for Sarah, with no sanitation, no water, and no electricity, and Topsy yearned for a different life away from the never-ending drudgery of her existence.

For the children, however, growing up at the foot of the mountain seemed like paradise, as they roamed across the fields and through the forests, splashed in the creeks and dammed streams with their friends from the neighbouring farms on their way home from the tiny country school in Maudsland, which their father had attended years before. In Gloria A Coghill's book

125 Years of Schooling in the Coomera,[75] there is an interview with Willie Campbell, the eldest of Bill and Topsy's children, in which he describes his school days.

> *"I remember when the virgin scrubs were cut and the hundreds of birds of all kinds flying out of the last fig tree to fall. Our countryside teemed with doves, pigeons and numerous other lovely birds and of course every burned-out tree stump would house a big carpet snake. Most of my schooldays were spent at Maudlsland State School. I remember my first day at school. My teacher was Mrs Westmann and I was terrified, so much so, my cousin Susie Bignell had to take me home. On my second day of school I hit Teddy Bignell on the nose and made it bleed because he held onto the tap of the school tank and wouldn't let me have a drink of water...*
>
> *With my best friend, my cousin Wally Bignell, we swam the river together, played endless cricket, ate enormous amounts of bananas at Mr Yaun's banana plantation plus anyone else's fruit growing in our vicinity, in fact we must have resembled a couple of flying foxes. It really was an idyllic childhood."*

Perhaps the children were too busy to notice the decline in their grandfather William; perhaps they were used to his bad temper and his eccentricities. By all accounts, in his later years William was not a pleasant man. By the time his fifth grandchild was born, William was already in his seventies, and his health, his patience and his mind were beginning to fade. Wrecked by decades of hard manual labour, he was still deeply affected by both the deaths of his first son at Ghinghinda and his dear wife Sarah twenty years later. Bill and Topsy had to make a heartrending decision. How they must have debated, discussed

---

75   *125 Years of Schooling in the Coomera*, Gloria A Coghill, Wongawallen, Queensland 1998, pp. 36–37.

and argued; how many tears must have been shed, how many cross words exchanged. Was it the right thing for William? Was it the right thing for them and the children? Perhaps William's health and state of mind left them no choice.

In 1922, while Topsy was pregnant with her sixth child, William Campbell was taken far from home and across Moreton Bay to North Stradbroke Island, and admitted to Dunwich Benevolent Asylum. He would never see his little farm again.

The precise medical reason for William's admission to the asylum is unknown, as under Queensland State laws, his records cannot be accessed until one hundred years from his death. For over eighty years, from 1865 to 1946, the asylum served the state of Queensland as a public institution for the elderly, the poor, the destitute, alcoholics and the chronically sick. Men outnumbered women, who were housed in separate wards, by almost six to one. It was always underfunded, and always understaffed. Able-bodied inmates were meant to staff the asylum themselves, but many were simply too elderly or infirm to assist. Up to the mid-1920s there were rarely more than twenty paid staff to look after around a thousand inmates.[76] Cheap labour was supplied by the local aboriginal population, right up until the asylum closed in 1946. Appallingly, only for the final twenty years were they paid, and only then after they took industrial action and petitioned the government; prior to that they received only rations.[77]

An article in the *Brisbane Courier* commented:

"Dunwich is a home rather than an asylum...although generally regarded as a retreat for the aged, well or infirm, it has become an asylum for the young also, for the inebriate, the epileptic, and some mental, cancer, and consumptive cases, elements that are undesirable amongst the old folk, although those seriously afflicted are segregated... There are serious cases which might well be placed in other and

---

76 www.stradbrokemuseum.com.au/dba
77 Ibid.

more suitable asylums, and which are allowed to mingle
more or less freely and indiscriminately with the inmates,
which is bitterly resented by the majority of the old folk."[78]

The inmates were housed in wards, or in a tented village in the grounds. Those who lived outside must have endured a difficult existence in the extremes of the Queensland climate. The asylum was served by a large general kitchen, a bakery, laundry, bath house, post office, library and reading room; there was also a barber's shop, a general store, and an entertainments hall with a stage.[79] Although inmates were allowed visitors, Brisbane was a three hour ferry ride away. How many could afford to make the journey? How many bothered? The author of the article noted with interest, *"the keenness of the inmates to keep in touch with the outer world"*. In reality, they were probably desperately homesick; for all intents and purposes, they were prisoners on their island home. So many of those poor old souls had already reached the end of the line by the time they were admitted to Dunwich. Having become a burden to their families and to society, they were simply abandoned there.

Those inmates who were well enough and had sufficient funds were sometimes allowed "back home" for holidays, provided of course they still had a "back home" to go to. The *Brisbane Courier* article records how,

"Many old folks return to the asylum much the worse for
their visits. It is pitiable to see such 'returns' – old men,
often sodden with drink, with filthy clothing, starved, sick
and penniless. These unfortunate beings are readmitted,
and after being bathed, shorn, freshly clothed, rested and
fed, in a few days are again happy and contented."[80]

---

78   *Brisbane Courier*, Tuesday 25th October 1927, www.trove.nla.gov.au
79   Ibid.
80   Ibid.

I do not know how often or indeed whether Bill Campbell ever made the journey to see his father in the asylum. With six small children and a farm to run, would he have had the time? Dunwich is not an easy place to get to, from anywhere. Did William pine for Tamborine? Was he lonely and confused by his new surroundings? Perhaps his health was such that he was glad of the rest and the care he received; maybe his mind was such that he no longer knew where or who he was, and no longer cared.

Bill did travel to Dunwich at the end of September 1926; when he returned on 2nd October, he brought back with him his father's body. William Campbell was buried in an unmarked grave in the little cemetery at Upper Coomera, just a few yards from where his beloved Sarah had been laid to rest fifteen years before.

The hardships that the people of Seaham endured throughout the 1920s and 1930s were echoed throughout the industrialised nations of the Empire, as the economic crisis in Britain reverberated across the world. The Australian economy began to sharply decline in the early 1920s, and by the middle of the decade the country was in severe recession. The London-based banks would no longer lend to a Queensland Labour government they considered to be too radical.[81] The Bank of England had advised the Australian state governments to make huge cuts to spending on public services and to cut wages to make exports more competitive. At the same time, the British financiers refused to allow the Australians to default on their loan agreements, and the country was crippled financially. As agriculture, the wool trade and mineral mining were affected by huge downturns in international markets, commodity prices fell sharply and businesses of all sizes shut down. By the late 1920s unemployment was already ten per cent, even before the Wall Street crash in 1929 sent the industrialised world hurtling into the most severe depression of modern times.

---

81   Queensland Historical Atlas, qhatlas.com.au/content/depression-era

Times had always been hard for the Campbells – did Topsy and Bill notice any significant difference to their income in the second half of the 1920s? Had their daily struggles to make ends meet become even more difficult? Dairy production was the one sector of the Queensland economy that had actually increased though the 1920s, and milk production had almost doubled between 1920 and 1930. There were around twenty family dairy farms on and around Tamborine Mountain and Upper Coomera after the First World War, and some of these were very successful, in particular those belonging to the Hollindales, the Birds and the Wilsons.

Topsy had never been content with the life of a farmer's wife, and had always dreamed of bigger and better things. She had spent her entire life looking after other people – her many younger brothers and sisters, her own six children, her husband and her elderly father-in-law. Her uncle Sam Bignell, who farmed the neighbouring land, had tried for years to persuade William Campbell to sell him his eighty acres, so that he could increase his own landholding and expand his successful dairy farm but the old man had always steadfastly refused. However, with his death, the way was clear for Topsy to put her plans into action, and in 1928 she finally persuaded Bill to sell their small farm to her uncle Sam.

Bill Campbell did very well out of the sale of his land, and was paid the sum of £1,600 (around £90,000 today). This must have seemed like a fortune at the time and, with cash to spend, Topsy and Bill looked around for a suitable new business venture in which to invest.

In early 1929, just as the country was about to plunge into the worst economic crisis in its history, the Campbell family left "Campbell's Mountain" for good. The wooden slab cottage with the tin roof that William Campbell had built for Sarah and their little boy was abandoned, fell into disrepair and was eventually demolished. The land that William had worked so tirelessly for years to clear of forest was swallowed up by the Bignell's dairy farm and, after thirty-five years, the Campbells were gone. Did Bill leave his friends and relations on the mountain with a heavy heart? Or was he glad to be leaving the endless toil of farm life for good, looking forward to a new adventure with his newly-gained prosperity? As his mother Sarah had done when she waved goodbye to her mother and sisters at Durham station over forty years before, Bill Campbell was about to change his future.

Topsy had always had a fancy for being the landlady of a busy hotel or public house. With no experience of the hospitality industry, and no experience of any business other than farming, in 1929 the Campbells purchased the lease on the Gunalda Hotel, a country pub with letting rooms out back. Topsy's ambitions were about to be fulfilled.

Gunalda lies northwest of the little country town of Gympie, a hundred and seventy miles north of Upper Coomera, far beyond Brisbane and on the edge of nowhere. Then home to around three hundred and fifty people, in the late 1920s and early 1930s, this was prime logging country, and the little town (in reality a small village) was the thriving centre of the local farming and forestry communities. Situated on the main north–south road that snaked down the eastern side of Queensland, it was a regular stop off point for the loggers and wagon drivers transporting timber and goods the length of the state.

Topsy revelled in her new role as chatelaine of the Gunalda Hotel. Every night she would be in the bar, laughing and chatting with the customers, the centre of attention. The children soon adapted to their new surroundings and quickly made friends. Topsy organised regular "themed" evenings and parties, and there was always a band playing on a weekend. The hotel was at the very centre of village life. A report from the *Maryborough Chronicle* of 15th June 1933 describes a "Highland Night" held at the hotel, hosted by Topsy of course, with the Maryborough Pipe Band, a dancing competition and prizes, attended by around twenty local couples. *"The function was a great credit to the organiser Mrs Campbell."*[82]

In reality, however, the hotel business was in trouble almost from the very beginning. A local newspaper report from January 1930 reveals that the Government Health Inspector had received complaints about the Campbells keeping pigs in the back yard of the hotel; he attended at the property and served an improvement notice, threatening prosecution if the animals were not removed. Bill and Topsy were farmers not business people and sadly things began to unravel for them fairly quickly. In November 1931 Bill was prosecuted for non-payment of taxes and was fined two pounds, plus three shillings and sixpence in court costs.

The Campbells had taken a huge gamble in selling the farm and purchasing the Gunalda Hotel, but their chances of making a success of their new business venture faded by the day as Queensland was gripped by the Depression, the decline in the economy speedy and aggressive. In June 1930, unemployment was already at almost twelve per cent; within the year it was over thirty per cent.[83] The government of the day was in dire straits and started selling off gold reserves to try to generate cash, in the face of huge political and social unrest. Many new immigrants who arrived during this time were treated with open hostility, especially those who had made the journey from Greece and Italy. There was an upsurge in radical politics, both on the far right and far left, with nationalist and fascist groups engaged in open confrontation with communists and socialists.[84] Tens of thousands of unemployed men travelled the length and breadth of the country looking for work; around sixty thousand people were on "susso", the state sponsored sustenance payment, which paid tiny amounts and was only available to those who had

82 *Maryborough Chronicle*, 15th June 1933, www.trove.nla.gov.au
83 Queensland Historical Atlas, qhatlas.com.au/content/depression-era
84 www.australia.gov.au/about-australia/australian-story/great-depression

already been out of work for months and who were often literally starving.

The Queensland government established work projects to attempt to alleviate the chronic unemployment throughout the state, including the building of roads, bridges and railway lines, the creation of public parks, gardens and sports grounds, as well as reforestation projects further north. One of the tourist roads to Tamborine Mountain was constructed via one of these schemes. Wages on the schemes varied hugely – a single man could be paid eleven shillings for a day's work; a man with a wife and seven or eight children would earn the same amount. Most of the work schemes were provided in and around Brisbane, and the smaller cities and larger towns in Queensland, but there was no nationwide coordination. The availability of work and the amount of pay varied from state to state, even city to city, and coverage was very patchy. In rural areas like Gunalda, there was very little help available, and many families were forced to rely upon charity although some were simply too proud to accept it, however drastic their circumstances.

Families were evicted from their homes and unemployment camps for homeless families were set up in parks and showgrounds. Many found themselves living in appalling squalor and poverty in shanty towns on the fringes of the cities. Women and children suffered the most, as many were simply abandoned as husbands and fathers took off to try to find work elsewhere; a fair few never bothered coming back. In Brisbane and other large centres of population, women resorted to whatever means possible to feed their children – theft, "fortune telling", pawning any valuables (and when they'd gone, their furniture) and of course prostitution, although there were far fewer men willing or able to pay for their services. It seemed supply exceeded demand, even in the "oldest profession".[85] On Tamborine Mountain, despite the hardships that many of them

85 "Making Ends Meet: Brisbane Women and Unemployment During the Great Depression", Joanne Scott, *Queensland Review*, 2006.

were enduring, the ladies of the Country Women's Association knitted and sewed clothes for desperate families, sending them off to charitable organisations for distribution in the city, or delivering them to individual families in need on and around the mountain.[86]

Children were often employed as cheap labour – many were taken out of school at twelve or thirteen, sometimes younger, but often found themselves out of work by the time they were eighteen when employers could no longer afford to pay them higher rates. There were always more children from desperate families only too glad to step into their shoes.

For five long and difficult years the Campbells persevered at the Gunalda Hotel, but with dwindling trade from the few wagons that passed, and the impoverished locals no longer able to afford to pop in for their customary beer, in 1934, Bill was forced to take on extra work as a wagon driver. Jimmy, the second youngest of the Campbell children, was taken out of school when he was not much more than ten, and sent off to work in a local dairy. He hated it, and eventually ran off and gradually made his way to Sydney where he worked in a factory from age sixteen. Jimmy had little contact with his parents thereafter, and their relationship became a strained one.

By the end of 1934, the Campbells realised that they were fighting a losing battle at the Gunalda Hotel. Unable to make a living and to pay off their numerous creditors, in early 1935, Bill and Topsy surrendered the lease and closed the doors on their dreams for the last time. Every single penny Bill had received from the sale of his parents' beloved farm at the foot of Tamborine Mountain, his inheritance, was gone. How he must have rued the day he agreed to sell to Sam Bignell.

The Campbells were penniless.

---

86 *The Turning Years, A Tamborine Mountain History*, Eve Curtis, North Tamborine, Queensland, 1998, p. 95.

18
Broken Threads

It is easy to look back upon the choices we have made during the course of our lives through the prism of hindsight. Sometimes we rejoice in the decisions and chances we took; perhaps we despair at the mistakes we made, the opportunities we failed to pursue, the risks taken, the words we said and the words we left unsaid. Many will have regrets; a lucky few of us will have none. A life lived in regret is no life at all. Regret distorts the memory of our past and the shape of our future.

Was Bill full of bitterness and regret at what his life had become? Or was he philosophical about his situation? As his life had begun to unravel, so the regular flow of letters to his cousin Edie began to slow down. Edie still wrote to Bill regularly, but without a reply. It is to her credit that she persevered with her correspondence in the absence of any response, particularly as she endured a spell of ill-health in the mid-1930s. She was also caring for her elderly mother, Fanny, who was becoming increasingly frail and frequently bedridden. But that was Edie – the battered old attaché case is full of happy memories of her various friends and relations, spanning decades. She was clearly very well thought of by all who knew her. Edie Threadkell was a dutiful daughter, niece and cousin, and a faithful and valuable friend, as her next door neighbours the Clydes would shortly discover.

By mid-1935, the Campbell family had become dispersed, disjointed and spread far and wide across the state of Queensland.

Bill had to resort to using the woodsman's skills he had learned as a very young man back in Upper Coomera. After travelling around for six months or so, taking jobs for a few weeks here, a few days there, he made his way to the tropical far north, seeking work as a timber cutter in the vast wilderness of the Atherton Tablelands, about a hundred miles south of Cairns. Timber cutting was considered the lowliest of trades – it was poor men's work – but Bill was desperate, and simply had no choice. It was timber cutting, or starve.

While living in a small logging camp in the midst of the rainforest, miles from anywhere, Bill resumed his correspondence with his cousin. Perhaps he was inspired by loneliness, perhaps by boredom, perhaps by regret. In two small brown envelopes, each with a Queensland postmark but with the stamps carefully cut out and preserved in some long-lost album, are two letters, sent from Bill to Edie in 1936. These two letters are all that remain from almost fifty years of correspondence between the two families, and provide a wonderful insight into the hardships Bill encountered, and his warm, affectionate relationship with the cousin he never met.

The first is dated January 27th, 1936.

"My Dear Cousin Edie,
I got your Xmas present the other day, it had been all over the State after me, thanks very much for remembering me.
I presume the photo is of yourself, if it is, you are looking very well, how is Aunt Fanny, well I hope. It is a long time since I heard of you and Aunty, I am damn well ashamed of myself for not writing to you, but I am a bad correspondent and am always in trouble about writing letters.
Well Edie, I have left the farm at Upper Coomera this last six years and have been wandering around Queensland a bit since and now I am in the north of Queensland, about 100 miles from Cairns, the biggest

*town in the north, I am right out in the Bush and hardly
see a soul. It is very lonely, I can tell you.*

*Mrs Campbell and two of the girls Kathleen and
Mary are in Cairns, Kathleen is working there, she was
18 years of age on Jan 18th last. Mary is the youngest she
is 11 years of age. Bill is the oldest boy he will be 22 next
March 24th, 1936. Jean is the next oldest, she is 21 years
of age. She is married now and has a boy and a girl. She
was married about 3 years ago, her name is Balkin. Her
husband's father is a storekeeper at a place called Gunalda
near Gympie. Just fancy me being a grandfather. Betty is
at Maryborough, she is 16 sixteen years of age, and Jimmy
is the other boy, he is 14 years of age, so there is all the
family, six of them, and two grandchildren.*

*Well Edie, how are all the folks in England. I am terribly
ashamed of myself for not keeping in touch with you, but
there it is, I never seem able to write at all. I am enclosing
a snap of myself so you can see what I look like now. I am
working in the timber here now, cutting walnut stumps for
veneer. It is what they call the Tableland Scrubs, it is a very
wet place, nearly always raining, right in the tropics.*

*…Write and tell me all the news about over there
when you get this, and I will try and keep in touch with
you after this, that verse on the calendar is a kick in the
pants for me alright, but in future I will remember.*

*Well my dear cousin, I will have to close as I am nearly
settled on what to write about, so will close with best of
love to you and Aunty, and a prosperous and Happy New
Year, although it is a little late, but better late than never,
with all the best wishes in the world,*

> *I remain, your loving cousin,*
> *W J Campbell"*

The letter says nothing about Jimmy's whereabouts – the truth
is Bill probably had no idea where his youngest son was at that

point. Enclosed were a number of small photographs, including one of Jean and her husband Jim Balkin, but mostly of Bill, showing him at work in the Tablelands. On the back of each, in Bill's distinctive handwriting, there is a description of his life and work as a timber cutter. Then in his mid-forties, he looks tired and resigned, perhaps even sad. On one of the photographs he has written, *"This is the class of work I do now"*, as though he were ashamed. And he was.

The second letter is dated May 10th, 1936.

My dear Aunt Fanny and Cousin Edie,
I received your welcome letter yesterday, and I can assure you both that I was very pleased to hear from you both, and that you were both as well as could be expected. I am sorry Edie that you are not in the best of health, as good health is the greatest blessing of all... Aunty is lucky that...you can help her, and that you are both together. That is the best of all, believe me I know, as my family and I are over 1000 miles apart and after been [sic] together for years it is no joke being separated.

I spent Easter with Topsy and Mary and Kathleen in Cairns, had a fortnight with them then came back to the Bush. They are all fairly well, Kathleen is the head barmaid at the Queens Hotel in Cairns, she gets £3 19s 0d per week, she has been there twelve months now. Topsy has been in Cairns for months now, and is going back down south soon, to visit the others, and I will go down next Xmas if all be well and I have enough cash.

I sold the farm in 1929, sold it fairly well too. Invested the money in a business just as the Depression started and went broke so am now out in the Bush, in North Qld, cutting timber, and trying to make a fresh start.

...You mention the heat, well Cairns in Summer is worse than hell, for Nov. Dec. and Jan. are always around the 100 degrees both night and day, the winter months from

April to September are nice and mild, the best in this part of the world, of course where I am on the Atherton Tableland 3000 feet above sea level, and a wonderful climate generally, only a cow of a place for rain. The wet season is generally from February to April, about 30 inches of rain a month for those months, and then occasional showers, about 130-150 inches each year. It is recognised as one of the wettest areas in the world, it is in the Tropics right enough.

Well if I praise the place any more you will think it is wonderful, but all I can say it is a damn shame they ever took it from the Blacks.

I think Topsy was going to write but she is like myself, not keen on writing, I will remind her to write.

Well, Aunt Fanny, I wish you would remember me to Aunt Emma and her family, and any of the others, of course never having seen them makes it hard to remember them, but I wish them all good luck and prosperity. Judging by the snap, Aunt Fanny looks really well, but Edie looks a lot thinner than the photo I got at Xmas, by the look of her on the seat at Redcar, she is in love and the boy has turned her down, never mind Edie, all's well that ends well, and you will have to come out here and get the Australian sun cure and settle down out here.

…I am enclosing a snap of Kathleen and myself walking down Abbott Street Cairns. It is a good one of both of us. I will try and get some of Topsy and the others and send you.

Well my dears, I think it is about time I close this scribble, hoping this finds both of you in the best of health and wishing you both the best of luck and love

From your loving xxxx Nephew and Cousin, otherwise Bill.

PS Be sure and write soon, don't do as I do but do as I tell you. I have received 3 bundles of papers from you, interested in days out here.

So long xxxx

Accompanying the letter is a photograph of Bill standing next to some of the timber he had cut. These weren't the sort of logs with which you or I would be familiar – they were huge, felled trees, some with a diameter of several feet, each one weighing well over a ton. There were massive kauri pines, grey gums, flooded gums, iron barks, bloodwoods, cedar and walnut, and countless other types of eucalyptus, cut using the "springboard method" which enabled a timber cutter to work above the massive thickened bases of the trees. A notch was chopped into the tree, and a board inserted into the notch, upon which the timber cutter stood, sometimes many feet in the air. There were no harnesses and no helmets. It was incredibly dangerous and brutally hard work, and the men endured extremely challenging conditions in the heat and wet of the tropics. Sometimes they lived in huts, but in the more remote locations they lived in tents, cooking their meals over open fires or on camp stoves. Occasional trips were made to the nearest settlement for food and supplies; Bill's nearest town was Ravenhoe, where he would go every couple of weeks or so, collecting his post from the Kerr Brother's Bakery and Store in the little main street.

The life of a timber cutter was fraught with danger; deep in the rainforests there were the usual hazards from snakes and spiders, but the very nature of the work itself rendered it one of the most dangerous occupations of the time. Just a few months after the second letter was written, Bill Campbell was involved in a terrible accident. He had been cutting walnut trees, which would be used to make veneers for furniture and pianos, when one of the logs he had cut and was loading onto a wagon rolled off and crushed him. It was a miracle that he was not killed outright, but he suffered severe injuries. He was never the same man. After months in and out of hospital in Cairns, and a spell with his daughter Jean in Gunalda, he eventually returned with Topsy to live in Brisbane, and they moved into a house in Given Terrace in the suburb of Paddington. Several of Bill's grandchildren remember visiting him there, and recall him as a very gentle soul. Bill's injuries were such that he was never able to work again, and he was constantly in and out of hospital.

By the time news of Bill's accident reached his cousin Edie in Seaham Harbour, she was already dealing with a grave situation much closer to home. In the autumn of 1937, just as the old Seaham Colliery streets began to be demolished and the residents rehoused on the new Parkside estate, her dear friend and next-door neighbour Lydia Clyde was taken ill. In early 1938, Lydia was admitted to hospital with chest pains, and a heart problem was diagnosed. Edie did what she could to help John, who was still a miner at Seaham Colliery, with the children – as well as young Lydia and Jack, there was now another little boy, George, who had been born in March 1932. At the end of April 1938, a month or so after little George's sixth birthday, Lydia died, aged forty-three, from a leaking heart valve, a condition which is so easily treated today. She was buried at Princess Road Cemetery a few days later. Alas, no trace of her grave remains. I spent hours stumbling around the cemetery looking for her, armed with the deeds to the plot John had purchased for them both, to no avail.

Edie and her mother were devastated at the loss of their neighbour. Young Lydia had to leave work to look after her younger brothers, and friends and neighbours rallied round to help, including Jim Groark, Lydia's boyfriend, whom she'd met at the age of fifteen when he worked as a grocer's boy at the Meadow Dairies. Jim and Lydia had become secretly engaged on her sixteenth birthday, and eventually married in April 1941 when Jim was home on leave from the Army. Jim Groark was my grandfather.

When Fanny Threadkell finally passed away in January 1940, just after wartime food rationing was introduced, the roles were reversed; young Lydia, Jack and little George were of great comfort to Edie, and she wrote regularly to Jim and Jack when they were called up to serve, Jim in the Royal Engineers and Jack in the Royal Air Force. She was incredibly proud of Jackie, as she called him, when he was presented with the Distinguished

Flying Medal by the King in 1943, after completing twenty-four bombing missions with Bomber Command. He was just twenty-one.

It is sometimes difficult for us to grasp the sense of community that existed in colliery towns and villages like Seaham throughout the 1920s and 1930s, and beyond. Your next-door neighbours, the people with whom you shared a back yard, a communal sink and a couple of outside toilets, or the people who lived opposite you across the coal-blackened back lane, criss-crossed with lines of clean washing, these people were your family. There existed a collective memory of shared hardships, poverty, industrial unrest, desperation in bad times, grief and anxiety in times of war. There was also the communal joy of street parties to celebrate a coronation or jubilee, the women of the street getting out their wool and knitting needles as soon as a pregnancy was announced, the traditional throwing of coins for the neighbouring children by a bride departing for church on her wedding day. For colliery folk, blood isn't always thicker than water. So it was with the Threadkells and the Clydes, and for this reason Edie was always considered by my family to be an "Aunt". She'd always been there – a friend to my great-grandmother, my grandmother, an auntie to my mother, my brother and me.

There were to be no more letters sent from Bill to Edie.

Bill Campbell finally succumbed to his injuries on 10th November 1942, at the age of just fifty, while his two boys, Willie and Jimmy, were serving with the ANZAC forces thousands of miles away. Jimmy had lied about his age to enlist, and spent his eighteenth birthday in a trench, under heavy fire, at the siege of Tobruk. I don't know if he ever saw his father again from the time he ran off to Sydney. Jimmy's wartime experiences (like those of Jim Groark and Jack Clyde) could fill another book.

Bill's granddaughter, Patsy, vividly recalls sorting sugar into brown paper bags with her mother Jean at the Balkin family store after Jean received the telephone call informing her of her father's death, tears streaming down her cheeks.

Edie always treasured the letters Bill wrote to her from the isolated logging camp in the Atherton Tablelands – they were the last she ever received from him. Edie never married; she had no children of her own. There was no one to listen to her stories of cousins in faraway places; no one to tell of the misfortunes that had befallen her grandfather, the Horsekeeper Thomas Marshall and his daughters, nor of the journey of the eldest, her aunt Sarah, from Seaton Village to the rainforests of Queensland.

Sarah's bravery, and the courage of thousands of other young women like her who left Britain under the Single Female Migrant Programme in the second half of the nineteenth century, have largely been forgotten. The uncertainty Sarah had faced when she first arrived in Brisbane, the struggles and tragedy she had endured at Ghinghinda, the industrial unrest she had encountered at Jondaryan, and the happiness she had found on her little farm at the foot of Tamborine Mountain, despite the floods and the droughts – all of this disappeared from the family memory. With Bill's death, the connection between Edie and the Campbells was broken; the gossamer thread which had connected Seaham and Queensland was cut.

Edie kept Bill's surviving letters, and all the photographs he and Topsy had sent, in her little box, her old attaché case, carefully placed together in small buff-coloured envelopes, on top of her parent's death certificates and her father's will, and amongst the numerous mementoes of her many friends and relatives. There they remained, for decades, occasionally glanced at while she was looking for something else, but nothing more, until a small, curious girl would ask to see the box whenever she visited her Aunt Edie.

It's a shabby, tattered old thing.

19

Full Circle

A grand passion can sometimes consume us, body and soul. That passion may be for the love of our lives, sometimes reciprocated, sometimes unrequited, sometimes unfulfilled through force of circumstance or a conspiracy of the fates. Perhaps that passion is for a place which inspires or calms us, a place we call home or a place to which we long to escape. Passion can so easily evolve into an obsession which invades every aspect of our existence, controls our thoughts and guides our actions. In some extreme instances, it erodes our free will and renders us incapable of making logical decisions. Common sense goes out of the window, and we are compelled to act upon impulse.

Sarah Marshall was, is, my obsession. I know Sarah. She knows me. She called, and I answered. I have no doubt that she wanted her story to be told, and that she chose me, the girl next door, to narrate it. The coincidences, the dog-eared copies of official documents, the faded family photographs, the fragile, handwritten letters, the snippets from long-obsolete newspapers, all led me in one direction. Driven by my passion for this forgotten woman, my path was fixed.

On a sunny Thursday morning in February 2017, I was awoken by birdsong. For a few moments, I lay listening to the sound of a stiff breeze playing through the leaves and the distant buzz of a wood saw. I arose and made myself a cup of tea, and slid open the glass doors onto the veranda. I paused, my teacup balanced on the rail, and I gazed at my surroundings, blinking in the dappled sunlight. I made my way down the wooden steps and across the lawn, still barefoot, and snuggled into the cushions on the garden swing.

In that moment, as I sipped my tea, I felt an overwhelming sense of calm and fulfilment, pure joy tempered with relief. The scent of freshly-mown grass and eucalyptus carried towards me on the breeze as I peered down through the towering silver-barked trees clinging to the mountain-side, past rolling wooded hills in every shade of green imaginable, shimmering in the heat. In the far distance, I could just make out the hazy turquoise of the Pacific Ocean, and I thought about the young servant girl from Seaton Village who had brought me from half a world away to Tamborine Mountain.

I had arrived in Brisbane in the midst of a forty degree heatwave a few days earlier, one hundred and thirty-one years and forty-two days after Sarah disembarked from the SS *Duke of Sutherland*. I reflected upon her arrival in the city on 30th December 1886, alone, apprehensive yet excited, bewildered yet determined. Unlike Sarah, I received the warmest of welcomes, from her great-granddaughter, Catherine Marsden. I spent my first morning with Catherine and her brother Gary Campbell Balkin, whose article about the Campbell family I had stumbled upon just twelve months previously, and whose knowledge and kindness have been of such help to me in the writing of this book. I sat with Gary and Catherine in a little cafe in Gary's apartment building overlooking the Botanic Gardens and I handed to them the small crumpled brown envelope, addressed to *"Miss Edith Threadkell, 6 Caroline Street, Seaham Harbour"* containing the letters and photographs sent by their grandparents Topsy and Bill Campbell to Edie and her mother a hundred years ago. The friendship between their family and mine, which had begun the day John and Lydia Clyde moved next door to the Threadkells in the turbulent summer of 1921, was rekindled. The threads which had connected the Campbells to Seaham, and which had been broken for over eighty years, were reconnected.

Brisbane shines. It is a city of water, glass, steel and light, carved in two by the Brisbane River which in turn is criss-crossed by ferryboats and footbridges. Little of the city Sarah knew remains, although the street names would be familiar – Charlotte Street, George Street, Roma Street, Kangaroo Point, Fortitude Valley. I was staying in an apartment building, which, by pure coincidence, was located just around the corner from Turbot Street where Sarah had lived and worked when she first arrived in the city and where it is likely that she met and fell in love with William Campbell.

Recovering from jet lag and a particularly nasty virus which had confined me to my bed for my first few days in Australia, I wandered out one evening at sunset and made my way to Turbot Street. Lined with tower blocks and office buildings, and with a stretch of the highway running through it, even at that time of day, it was incredibly busy. Face-painted rugby fans from all over the world – New Zealand, South Africa, Samoa, France and even Japan – were heading back to their hotels with their flags and banners after the Brisbane Tens Tournament.

At the corner of the street, opposite a couple of Seven-Eleven stores which seemed to sell nothing but sun hats, nachos and Gatorade, I spotted the old Dispensary Building, and beyond it the alleyway from where the unfortunate Peter Bertram had been chased by Sammy, the escapee tiger from Higgins' Menagerie, before being rescued by Mr Higgins and Valentine Spendlove in October 1888.

As darkness fell, the heat was unremitting, stifling, suffocating.

I retraced my steps and followed the bend of the river down the length of William Street, to the site of the William Street Depot where Sarah had registered with the authorities and where she had lodged in the single women's dormitory for her first few days until she had secured employment. From the outside, the Victorian building is little changed; inside, it now houses office space and an architects' practice.

From my vantage point in my apartment on the nineteenth floor of Brisbane's tallest building, with its bird's eye view of the river and the South Bank, I sat on the floor by the window and watched as the sky darkened and a biblical storm rolled in. It encircled the city with a crown of thunderclouds, adorned with lightning flashes. And then the rain began. I had never witnessed anything like it. I have never seen rain fall in such volume and such force for such a length of time. I watched the rush-hour commuters hundreds of feet below me dash into doorways to avoid the deluge and I thought about the cyclone and the deadly floods that had swept through Brisbane just weeks after Sarah's arrival. How terrified she must have been.

The following day I left the heat and hustle and bustle of the city behind and headed south on the main highway, past the endless car dealerships, anonymous housing developments and retail outlets, past signposts for towns and villages which seemed almost familiar – Logan, Beenleigh, Gold Coast, Surfer's Paradise, Coomera. I pulled off the highway just south of Logan and immediately the landscape was transformed.

In no time at all I was in farming country, surrounded by gentle hills and agricultural land interspersed with eucalyptus forest, yellow diamond-shaped road signs warning me to be on the lookout for koala and wallabies. I saw neither, but suddenly as I rounded a bend, there it was, between the trees. I recognised the downward sweep and the silhouette of Tamborine Mountain immediately, and tears stung my eyes. The narrow road twists and winds steeply upwards, and feels almost perpendicular in places. I found myself in the depths of the rainforest, amongst towering palms and huge, dense ferns, the sky barely visible through the canopy.

Upon reaching the mountain plateau, the landscape changes again, with a sunny, open aspect. Away from the trashy tourist shops and cafes of Gallery Walks at the northern end of the mountain, the main road snakes southwards, past vineyards and discreetly expensive houses, hidden amongst beautifully manicured gardens at the end of long tree-lined drives.

I fell in love with Tamborine Mountain.

I was bewitched by the natural beauty of the place, the restful, quiet atmosphere, and the gentle climate, so different from the heat and the hassle of Brisbane. I felt so at home in the little main street at North Tamborine, with its lovely coffee shops frequented by the locals. Unassuming, friendly, nothing fancy – much like the locals themselves, who extended to me the warmest of welcomes, and could not have been more helpful when they discovered the reason for my visit.

On the eastern side of the mountain, past the golf course, looking towards the Pacific and the distant high rises of Gold Coast, down a very steep and treacherous road, and tucked away at the bottom of a wooded drive, I discovered what I was looking for, the very spot I had travelled ten thousand miles to find. With the help of Ian Hollindale, the grandson of Topsy's younger sister Ivy Bignell, whose family still own the land next door, I finally stood on the land that Sarah and William had purchased all those years ago.

Beyond the wooden fence at the edge of the property lies a small creek, surrounded by trees, beneath which a handful of sheep were grazing. For a brief moment I closed my eyes, and in that moment, I knew; Sarah had loved this place. She had found peace and happiness here. I wondered just how Bill and Topsy could ever have parted with the farm, and how they must have longed to return here, when all was lost.

I continued down the mountain to Upper Coomera and paused at the little park at river's edge which commemorates the man who built the jetty there. I stood at the spot where Siganto's Wharf had once been, where Sarah and William had first arrived on the Coomera. Here they had disembarked from the packet steamer with all their worldly goods; in later years, William visited the busy little wharf every day, collecting deliveries in his horse and cart.

Upper Coomera today is pleasant enough, especially down by the river, but eventually the fields give way to the creeping urbanisation that is Coomera – endless new housing estates and out-of-town shopping outlets, a theme park, and the very exclusive, eye-wateringly expensive waterside residential developments of Sanctuary Cove and Hope Island.

In the baking stillness of a late February day, I said goodbye to Tamborine Mountain and made my way up the Bruce Highway which runs down the eastern coast of Queensland, connecting Brisbane with tropical Cairns in the far north. The highway is, for much of its one thousand and twenty-six mile length, single carriageway, and winds its way over creeks and rivers, past mountain ranges and through towns and villages of various sizes including Maryborough, Rockhampton, Mackay and Townsville.

One thousand and twenty-six mile miles. If I was to travel that far from Seaton Village I would be on the Poland-Belarus border. The Bruce Highway is notorious as one of the world's most dangerous highways, allegedly responsible for a huge seventeen per cent of all of Australia's road fatalities, mainly due to aggressive overtaking but also poor maintenance and frequent flooding. Stretches of the road are poker straight, for mile after monotonous mile, testing the powers of concentration of even the most conscientious driver, who may all too easily drift into the path of one of the huge logging trucks that thunder southward.

With this cheery thought in mind, I left the very upmarket seaside resort of Noosa where I'd decided to stay for a few days, and joined the highway just west of the market town of Eumundi. I headed north-west, past the pyramid-like Mount Cooroy and the picturesque rolling farmlands of the Mary Valley, and the numerous agricultural machinery suppliers on the outskirts of the old-fashioned town of Gympie. I continued my journey northwards, towards my destination, the small town of Gunalda, and in particular, the Gunalda Hotel. Amazingly, it's still there, and still serving customers, eighty-three years after Bill and Topsy Campbell were forced to surrender the lease, penniless, their hopes and dreams in tatters.

I turned off the Bruce Highway towards Gunalda, which the signposts indicated was just a short distance away. Tasteful roadside advertisements for the hotel appeared at regular intervals. Gunalda isn't a one-horse town. It's not even a half-horse town. This was the back of the back of beyond. Once a thriving little place that served the surrounding rural communities and the wagon drivers on main north–south route, there is very little of note left now. When the Bruce Highway was built, the traffic no longer passed so close to the town, and slowly it began to die.

Today, Gunalda principally consists of two streets set at a right angle, a bakery, a second-hand store, an estate agents, a shop which doubles as a post office, and beyond that, the hotel. I called into the post office as I needed to send a parcel to Jimmy Campbell's son Bob in Toowoomba. It sold everything from vegetables to table lamps to flip flops to wooden chickens to condoms to saws to ACDC t-shirts to flags, and reminded me a lot of the shop in Seaton Village, Seaton Supply Stores, as it was when I was growing up.

I left the post office and walked the few yards to the Gunalda Hotel. The very name conjures up images of genteel accommodation in the colonial style, potted palms swaying in the breeze on the veranda, guests sporting panama hats and expensive shoes sipping daiquiris on the lawn. A sort of Queensland version of the "Raffles Hotel" in Singapore.

"Hotel" was stretching it. A great deal. The establishment in which I now found myself was straight out of a television advert for Australian beer. It was a low, one storey building, attached to an older construction with a wrap-around porch (which I assumed housed the letting rooms), with a large sign bearing the words "Great Northern Brewing Co – Gunalda Hotel".

The interior was strangely modern but dark and incongruous, totally devoid of character, the original fixtures and fittings having been removed long since. At the bar sat a couple of bearded locals. Both were covered in tattoos and sported double denim and sunglasses, and glared at me as I ordered my lunch. Neither spoke. I tried to imagine the hotel back in the early 1930s, busy, noisy, crammed with locals, a band playing in the corner, Topsy holding court in the bar and Bill avoiding the limelight as always, changing the barrels out back.

I ate my lunch under the sometimes curious, sometimes hostile gaze of the locals. Still no one spoke. Still they continued staring. This was the one and only occasion I felt uncomfortable on my entire trip, and I beat a hasty retreat.

Sadly, I did not have time to drive the hundreds of miles into the outback to see Ghinghinda, the place where James Campbell had drowned and where Sarah's heart had been broken. Nor had I been able to visit Jondaryan where Bill Campbell had been born, nor the Atherton Tablelands where he had laboured as a logger, an occupation that had ultimately cost him his life. Nothing can prepare you for the sheer vastness of Australia; I could have travelled around Queensland for a year and still not have seen all the places where the members of the Campbell family had lived, worked and died.

Before returning to Seaton Village, there was one last place I was compelled to visit. I couldn't contemplate going back home without seeing it, and yet the prospect of doing so filled me with an odd mixture of dread and anticipation. Even as I pulled my car into the small car park, the gravel crunching and spitting beneath the wheels, I felt a growing knot of apprehension in the pit of my stomach. I walked through the gates and across the neatly-manicured lawns, past the shrubbery and the gardener with his grass cutter, who nodded a "good morning".

It was exactly how I had imagined it.

I paused for a moment, before kneeling down by the low wrought-iron railings, now rusted and shabby, the white paint long since peeled away. I leant forward and brushed my fingertips against the rough edges of the weather-worn headstone, which had broken off from its plinth, and was resting back against the railings. Despite the passage of a century and several lifetimes, the inscription remained clearly legible. I smiled and whispered, one County Durham girl to another,

"Hello Sarah. I'm here."

Bibliography

Books

Bean, CEW *On The Wool Track* (Angus & Robertson) Great Britain
1910

Bryson, B *Down Under* (Transworld Publishers) Great Britain 2000

Curtis, E *The Turning Years - A Tamborine Mountain History* (Privately
Published) North Tamborine 1988

Devries, S & J *Historic Brisbane - Convict Settlement to River City*
(Boolarang Press) Brisbane 2013

Elliot & Derrick - *Letters to Boondall 1872-1879*, and Lena Cooper's
Manuscript (Boolarang Publications) Southport 1993

Fox, M J *Fox's History of Queensland* 1919 -1923 (States Publishing
Co.) Brisbane 1923

Fuerbringer, W FIPS *Alarm! Tauchen!(: U-Boot in Kampf und Sturm*
(Ullstein) (Berlin) 1933

(translated by G Brooks, 2000)

Gothard, J *Blue China* (Melbourne University Press) Melbourne 2001

Government of Queensland *Queensland Past and Present: 100 years
of statistics* 1896-1996 Ch. 8 Section 5 pp 263-270 (Government
Statistician's Office) Brisbane 1998

Grant, E *Memoirs of a Highland Lady* (John Murray) Edinburgh 1898
Canongate Books Ltd/ Andrew Tod 1988

Haines, R *Life and Death in the Age of Sail* (National Maritime
Museum) London 2003

Hollindale, I *Life and Cricket on the Coomera* (Privately Published)
Gold Coast 2008

Hughes, R *The Fatal Shore* (Vintage) Australia 1986

McCutcheon, J *Troubled Seams* (Privately Published) Seaham 1955

Rudd, Steele *On Our Selection* (Bulletin) Sydney 1899

Walker, J *Jondaryan Station* (University of Queensland Press) Brisbane 1988

Woolcock, R *Rights of Passage* (Tavistock Publications Ltd) London 1986

Academic Papers/Published Articles

Balkin, GC "Putting War Horror in Past Took Love and Work" *New Farm Village News*, December 2015

Callaghan, J "Case Study" *Brisbane Cyclone* 1887 (Harden Up Queensland, date unknown)

Chesterfield, R "The Growth and Expansion of the Durham Miners' Association" (Part 2) www.durhamintime.org.uk (date unknown)

Crook, DP "Aspects of Brisbane Society in the 1880s" (Thesis) 1958 University of Queensland

Curtis, E "A Land of Hills and Valleys Tamborine Mountain 1874–1914" (Queensland Heritage, Undated)

Devaney, J "Tambourine – Its Early History" *Brisbane Daily Mail* 24th December 1928

Durham County Record Office GS Boggin Scrapbooks UD/Sea pp 48–49

Emmett, S "Looking Back on Old Brisbane" (notes for address delivered at the meeting of the Historical Society of Queensland 22nd July 1954)

Linsley, S Extracts from Lecture Notes (undated)

Murphy, C Campbell Family History (undated)

Our Brisbane History – 1916 A Nation Divided – Conscription 2009 ourbrisbanehistory.blogspot.co.uk/2009/10/

Queensland Country Life – Jondaryan, Last of the Big Downs Stations (National Library of Australia) 10th January 1946

Reid, G "From Hornet Bank to Cullin-a-Ringo" (Presented to the Royal Historical Society of Brisbane 24th May 1981)

Renshaw, P "Black Friday 1921" *History Today* Vol.21 Issue 6th June 1971

Scott, J "Making Ends Meet: Brisbane Women and Unemployment in the Great Depression", *Queensland Review*, 2006

The Spectator Archive (Author Unknown) "The End of the Miners' Strike 1st July 1921" www.archive.spectator.co.uk

Newspaper Archives

Australian Newspapers accessed via www.trove.nla.gov.au

Beaudesert Times

Brisbane Courier

Brisbane Telegraph

Clarence & Richmond Advertiser and New England Examiner

Maryborough Chronicle

Newcastle Morning Herald & Miners' Advocate

Rockhampton Morning Bulletin

Sydney Morning Herald

Sydney Evening News

The Times of London (via Durham Mining Museum www.dmm.org.uk)

Websites

ancestry.co.uk

ancestry.com

archive.spectator.co.uk

awm.gov.au/atwar/ww1

durhamatwar.org.uk

east-durham.co.uk/seaham/timeline

England Census 1871, 1881, 1891, 1901, 1911

findmypast.com

historytoday.com/patrick-renshaw/black-friday-1921

Queensland State Archives – Passenger Lists www.slq.qld.gov au/
resources

themcwhirtersproject.com – Man Eating Tiger Eats Man on George
St Brisbane 1888

trove.nla.gov.auuboat.net/wwi/commanders/81.html